CW01333045

TURKEY
A PICTURE MEMORY

Text
Bill Harris

Captions
Fleur Robertson

Design
Teddy Hartshorn

Photo Editor
Annette Lerner

Editorial
David Gibbon

Photography
Colour Library Books Ltd.
FPG International

Director of Production
Gerald Hughes

CLB 2793
© 1992 CLB Publishing, Godalming, Surrey, England
All rights reserved.
This 1993 edition published by Magna Books,
Magna Road, Wigston, Leicester, England
Colour separations by Scantrans Pte Ltd, Singapore
Printed and bound by Tien Wah Press (PTE) Ltd, Singapore
ISBN 1-85422-560-X

TURKEY
A PICTURE MEMORY

MAGNA BOOKS

Black Sea
Edirne
Istanbul
Bosphorus
Sea of Marmara
Dardanelles
Izmit
Adapazari
Zonguldak
Karabük
Samsun
Batumi
Tbilisi
Trabzon
Bursa
Balikesir
Lesbos
Sakarya
Eskisehir
Ankara
Kizilirmak
Kirikkale
Manisa
Izmir
Afyon
Aegean
Sea
Büyük Menderes
Denizli
TURKEY
ANATOLIA
Tuz Gölü
Sivas
Kayseri
Seyhan
Konya
Antalya
Taurus
Rhodes
Mersin
Adana
Iskenderun
Iskenderun Körfezi
Antakya
Halab
Gaziantep
Urfa
Malatya
Diyarbakir
Tigris
Euphrates
Erzurum
Jerevan
ARMENIA
Van Gölü
KURDISTAN
Al Mawsil
Mediterranean Sea
Cyprus

First page: Istanbul's medieval Blue Mosque at sunset, and (previous page) the village of Narince in central Turkey.

What potential visitors contemplating a trip to Turkey often expect to find is an exotic setting out of the *Arabian Nights,* with decadent men presiding over nightly debauches in mysterious harems, and the potential danger of Byzantine intrigues that could end in sudden death or slavery for the unwary. They are invariably disappointed. Even more sophisticated travelers are sometimes disarmed by the friendliness, patience and understanding they find among their Turkish hosts. But that is one of the old traditions that hasn't been swept away with the past. Since ancient times, the Turks have used the term *tanri misafari* to describe visitors. Roughly translated it means "God's guest," a designation everyone in Turkey has always taken very seriously. On the other hand, it is a rare visitor whose imagination doesn't conjure up exotic images of a glittering past, when Turkey was the center of not one, but two of the richest and most powerful empires anywhere in the world. There are reminders of them everywhere.

The history spread out over the Turkish landscape goes back some 10,000 years. The ancient Hittites flourished there, as did the Phrygians, led by the legendary King Midas. The Lydians under King Croesus created the world's first money, which may help explain why so many other peoples invaded and populated the region known as Anatolia, now the heart of modern Turkey. Among them were the early Greeks, whose culture blossomed along the Aegean coast long before Athens became the center of their world.

Their most important city on the coast, which they called Smyrna, was established by the Aeolians, who were eventually forced out by their cousins the Ionians, who in turn lost it to the Lydians. The city itself was destroyed in the process, but it was rebuilt by Alexander the Great who, according to legend, was visited in a dream by a goddess who told him to do it. The local villagers confirmed Alexander's vision by consulting an oracle and went to work, and there has been a city on the spot ever since. Today it is known as Izmir, and anyone visiting there must wonder why anyone needed the advice of a goddess or an oracle to figure out that it is a perfect spot for a city. It sits at the end of a long gulf, with easy access to the interior. The land around it is rich and fertile, and the climate is close to perfect, with plenty of rainfall, but only during the rainy season at the beginning of the year. The summers are hot, but sea breezes make them pleasant, and it is obviously not for nothing that people have been living there since the third millenium B.C.

In the Roman era, Smyrna was known to them as the most beautiful city in the world, after Rome, of course, and writers were especially enthusiastic about her paved streets, a rare thing in Greek cities. They also wrote of a local shrine to the Greek poet Homer, and said that it marked the spot where he was born.

Many other cities have claimed Homer as a native son, but it wasn't until the last century, when it was proven that he was a historian and not just a spinner of tall tales, that scholars began searching in earnest for his origins. And today most agree that Smyrna was most likely his home town. The man who rekindled the interest was Heinrich Schliemann, who used the poet's writings as his guide in a search for ancient Troy and found it in Aegean Turkey in 1871.

Schliemann found not one but four ancient towns on the site, and later excavations unearthed five more, suggesting that settlement there dated back to the Bronze Age. The one Homer wrote about existed from 1800 to 1275 B.C., when it was destroyed by an earthquake. Homer said that the city had been under siege by the Achaeans for ten years in an effort to recapture Helen, the kidnapped wife of the Spartan King Menelaus. The siege ended, according to Homer, when Ulysses came up with the idea of entering the city by presenting it with a wooden horse which, unknown to the Trojans, was full of soldiers. If there really was such a horse, Schliemann wasn't able to find any trace of it, but he did find evidence of the earthquake, and concluded that it had damaged the city walls and allowed the Achaeans to march in with or without one. And because he had complete faith in Homer as a historian, he also concluded that they probably built a huge replica of Poseidon's horse as a symbol of gratitude to the sea god who was believed to be the one who caused earthquakes.

There are all kinds of ways to take a city. When King Attalus III of Pergamum died in 133 B.C. he bequeathed his city, known as Bergama, to the Romans, who added it to their empire without the loss of a single soldier and used it as a springboard for expanding their influence into the East. But they got a lot more than a magnificent city with strategic importance. Within its walls was a library containing some 200,000 volumes, second in all the world only to the one at Alexandria in Egypt. The Pharaoh had tried to maintain his position as custodian of the world's knowledge by prohibiting the export of papyrus, but the Pergamenes responded by perfecting the Ionian art of writing on animal skins, which eventually became known as parchment. In time it made papyrus obsolete, and because it was too stiff to be put on rollers it led to the development of bookbinding.

Ironically, the Pergamene library was dismantled and taken to Alexandria as a gift from Antony to Cleopatra. It was destroyed in the seventh century, along with most of the original Egyptian texts, by a zealous Muslim caliph who decided that any book not consistent with the teachings of the Koran should be removed from the world. The original building that housed the collection at Bergama is being restored by German archaeologists, following in the footsteps of their predecessors who began uncovering the secrets of the old city a century ago.

At about the same time that German scientists began exploring ancient Pergamum, other secrets about the same corner of Asia Minor were being uncovered in a decidedly unscientific way back in Germany. A woman named Catherine Emmerich, who had been bedridden for a dozen years and had never been outside Germany, wrote a book on the life of the Virgin Mary. She accurately described a mountainside near Ephesus, as well as a house she said was where the Virgin had lived the last years of her life. In 1891 an expedition following her directions found the spot exactly where she said they would. The house was immediately converted into a chapel and became the focus of Christian pilgrimages. Before then, it was accepted that the mother of Christ had remained in Jerusalem, where she died at the age of 63. An early Church Council concluded that she had at least visited Ephesus with St. John, but it was more a matter of faith than proven fact, although when St. Paul arrived there in 53 A.D. he was surprised by the number of Christians he found among the Ephesians.

Turkey has dozens of sites venerated by the Christians and Jews, and is often called "the first province of God after Jerusalem." Places within modern Turkey are mentioned throughout the Bible, from the landing place of Noah's Ark on Mount Ararat to Abraham's home in Harran and the seven churches in Asia Minor that inspired the Revelation of St. John. But if Christianity began its spread into the world from there and it is prominent in Jewish tradition, Christians and Jews account for only about one percent of Turkey's population. The rest are Muslims.

Islam arrived there on May 29, 1453, when Sultan Mehmet II entered Istanbul's Sancta Sophia, the biggest church in all Christendom, and announced that it was reserved for himself. The great building, whose name translates as The Church of Holy Wisdom, became a mosque at that same moment. The building was nearly a thousand years old by then. The city itself had been a center of civilization for twice as long.

Tradition says that the original city, called Byzantium, was founded by Greeks in the seventh century B.C. In its early years it was successively overrun by nearly every warring culture within striking distance, and in about 150 B.C. it became a part of the Roman Empire. It had faded into near insignificance by the fourth century A.D., when the Roman Emperor Constantine decreed that a new city worthy of the name "New Rome" should be built on the site. When it was dedicated six years later, it was considered worthy of an even better name: Constantinople, the city of Constantine.

The Roman Empire had already been divided in two, and Constantinople was the center of the eastern portion. Its importance was enhanced by the fact that Constantine had been converted to Christianity and was instrumental in establishing the religion in Europe. His great city became a mecca for Christians, largely because of the great number of holy relics that had been assembled there by Constantine's mother, St. Helena.

The glory of Rome itself came to an end with the Barbarian invasions of 475 A.D., but the Eastern empire continued. It would eventually become more powerful than Rome had ever been, and its influence over the world as the Byzantine Empire would last a thousand years. Its foundations were laid by the Emperor Justinian, who had embarked on a self-imposed mission to rule over the entire Mediterranean world. It was an expensive undertaking, and when his people rebelled against him, destroying the center of his Imperial City in the process, he countered by ordering it rebuilt into a showplace that would replace their discontent with patriotic pride. He created dozens of new churches, including the glorious Sancta Sophia, as well as scores of imposing public buildings, and rebuilt the Grand Palace, a group of buildings he and his wife, the Empress Theodora, called home.

The spread of Islam began less than a century later, and in an incredibly short time Arab armies had overrun Persia, Egypt, Syria and Carthage. The key to their success was their powerful navy, and the key to stopping it was the defenses of Constantinople. The Arab fleet attacked time after time, and each time it was turned away by a secret weapon the Byzantines called Greek fire, a substance that burst into flames on contact. Even if it missed a ship it burned fiercely on the water, terrifying sailors. The secret of Greek fire has never been revealed even to this day, but it was powerful enough to stop the march of Islam toward the west.

By the beginning of the eleventh century, there was no city in the world that compared to Constantinople, by any measure. Her population was completely international, her wealth incredible, and her architectural treasures made the city the most opulently-beautiful thing ever created by man. It was only natural that it should be a target of the Crusaders, who claimed they were only interested in freeing the holy places of Christendom but saw Byzantium as a prize worth fighting for. It wasn't until the Fourth Crusade in 1204 that the Western knights were able to take the city, and by then they had apparently forgotten some of the principles they had been fighting for. After slaughtering their fellow Christians, they systematically robbed the churches of art and relics, much of which is still quite proudly displayed in the great Cathedrals of Europe. The bronze horses that had graced the Hippodrome were carried off to Venice, and other priceless examples of Byzantine art were scattered to other parts of the world. They divided the territory among the powers of Venice, Rome and Greece and exiled the emperor, and Constantinople became a shadow of its former self. Almost everything of any value had been carried off and the city seemed beyond repair. The Byzantines retook Constantinople fifty years later, but then there was another force for them to contend with.

A warlord named Osman had begun establishing the Ottoman Empire and, though Greek fire kept him at arm's length, the people of Constantinople saw their own former empire reduced to little more than the city itself. The Ottoman Turks seemed content to let matters rest there, but when Mehmet II became their sultan in 1451, he managed to surround Constantinople and keep it under siege. The Byzantine emperor lodged a formal protest, but the Turks ignored it. He turned next to the Pope in hopes that he would send his armies to turn away the threat, but instead the Pontiff sent a Cardinal, who said mass in Sancta Sophia and then went back to Rome. In a matter of weeks Mehmet II rode through the streets of Constantinople in triumph.

But, unlike the Barbarians who sacked Rome and the Christians who ruined Byzantium, the Muslims went right to work restoring the city. Mehmet allowed the Christians to keep their religion, although he converted most of their churches, including Justinian's Sancta Sophia, into mosques. He also built himself an impressive palace, Topkapi Sarayi, which was expanded and enhanced by every sultan who followed him until the 1830s, and is now one of the world's great museums, a place where visitors say they can still feel the presence of the sultans and their courts.

The Ottoman Sultanate lasted until 1923, when the Republic of Turkey was born, and there are monuments to the man who made it happen in nearly every Turkish city and town. His name was Mustafa Kemal. When he was born in Salonika in 1881, it was customary for Muslims to be known only by their given names, but he added "Kemal" to his when one of his teachers gave him the name, which means "excellence," in recognition of his classroom accomplishments. Many years later, when the law was changed to require family surnames, the Turkish Parliament gave him a new one, "Attaturk," which means "Father Turk."

Kemal had been a leader in the secret society known as the Young Turks which succeeded in overthrowing the Sultan Abdul Hamid II in 1909 and became a part of the new government, which in his opinion was no better than the one it replaced because it refused to sweep away old ideas. In spite of his opposition to the government and the war, he became world-famous as a general during World War I, when his defeated troops from Britain, Australia and New

Zealand at the Battle of Gallipoli. Turkey had fielded more than a million-and-a-half men in support of the Germans during the war, and when it was over the country was occupied by the Allied powers. Kemal turned the occupation into an opportunity by forming a government in exile in Ankara, even though Istanbul was Turkey's official capital, where the Sultan ruled as a puppet of the Allies. Kemal's government also controlled a nationalist army that gave a good account of itself against the Greeks in a three-year war that began in 1919, and when it was over, he had won the power to renegotiate the treaties of the World War and replace the Sultan with what he called the Sultanate of the People, which led to the creation of the Republic. When it was established, most of the best-informed world leaders believed it was futile gesture. In a single generation, Turkey had seen crushing military defeats, an outward migration of its brightest people, the financial drain and human cost of a world war, and a foreign occupation bent on carving it up into irretrievable pieces.

But Mustafa Kemal believed passionately in his people and their heritage. He told them that their future was in their own hands and that tearing down their old traditions would free them to reclaim the best of them and reform the others. The response was as inspiring as the message itself. No country in the history of the world has ever moved as quickly toward change as Turkey in the 1920s. For the first time, long before such an idea was acceptable in the West, women were given the same rights as men. Western-style clothing replaced costumes that had distinguished one class from another. The beautiful, but difficult to read, Arabic alphabet was replaced by Latin characters, and in less than six months every adult citizen was enrolled in a school, learning to read them, virtually eliminating illiteracy. Kemal also established a new banking system and reformed the government bureaucracy, and before he died in 1938, he had made Turkey a part of the Western world. It was a transformation that required an incredible amount of persuasion, and in most leaders the challenge would almost certainly be met by establishing a dictatorship. But Ataturk and his people had seen enough of that to know there had to be a better way. He spent his days sharing a dream with the Turkish people and convincing them that their future depended on following it. The key to it, he told them, was to become a part of the West rather than an outpost of it, and in the years since the Turks have never lost sight of the goal.

But if everything has changed in Turkey in the last fifty years, the past is still very much alive and very much a source of pride, although the Turks are proudest of all of the recent past and what has been accomplished in their own lifetimes. Why it has all worked so well was explained long ago by a Turkish philosopher who defined happiness by saying: "When God wants a man to be very, very happy, he makes him lose his donkey and then lets him find it again."

Facing page: the cobbled mountain road from Kâhta to Nemrut Dağ, in the province of Adıyaman.

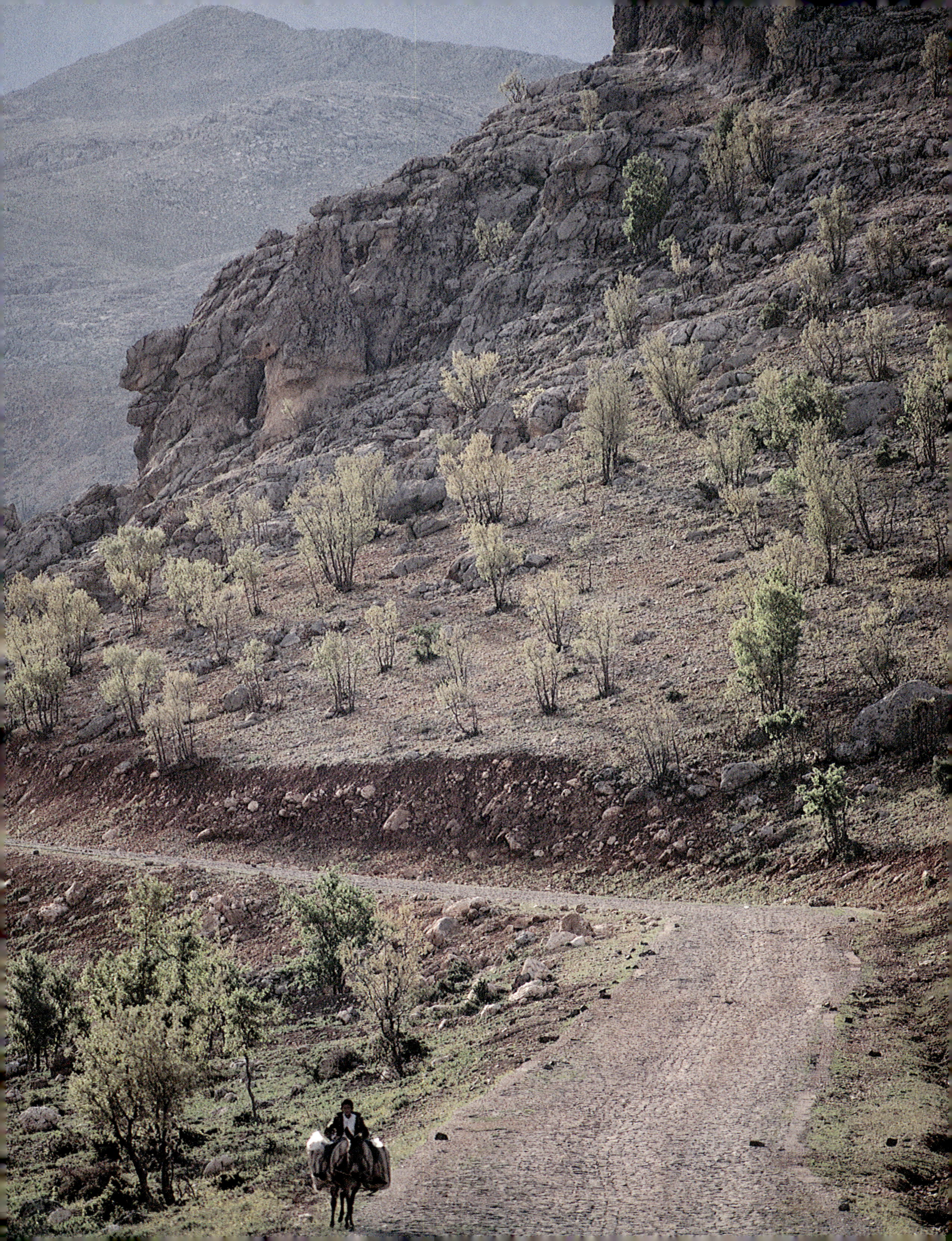

10

Nemrut Dağ (left) is one of the best known historical sites east of Ankara. Lying astride the summit of a mountain near Kâhta is the burial site of an insignificant king called Antiochus, who ruled central Turkey in the first century AD. Ten colossal statues of five gods are to be found here, one of whom is Antiochus himself, bent on self-glorification, while Zeus, Heracles and Apollo are among the others. Five face towards the sunrise, five towards sunset and all have been separated from their torsos over the years. Antiochus found the silhouette of Nemrut Dağ aesthetically lacking, so he had it increased in height by 150 feet with the addition of loose stones. All that is here had to be dragged up the mountain – the highest in the kingdom – by Antiochus' subjects. The view from the top (below) was probably unappreciated by them, though it is much loved by visitors today. Remaining pictures: the walls of Diyarbakir on the Tigris River, which date from 330-500 AD., and (overleaf) the Euphrates near Kâhta.

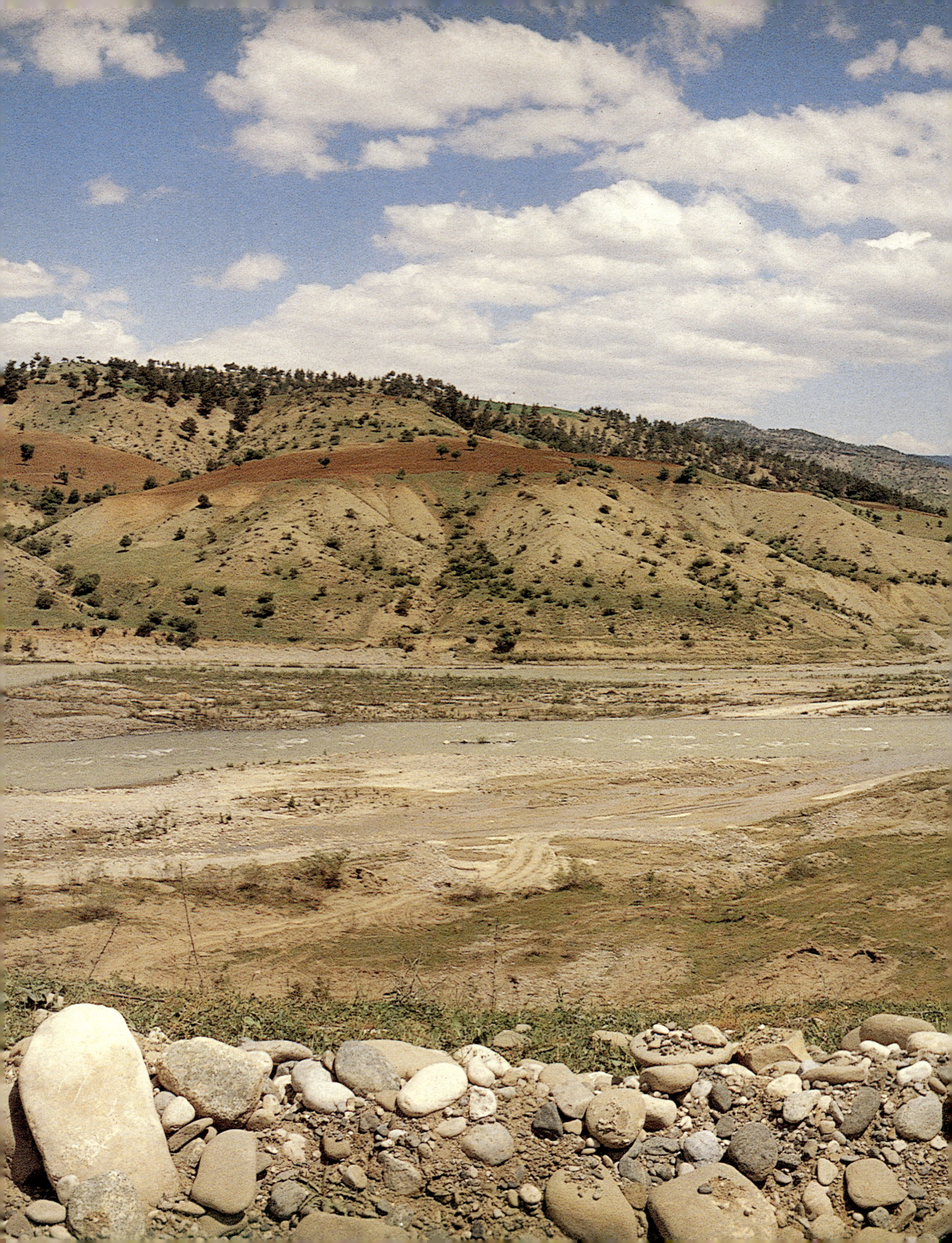

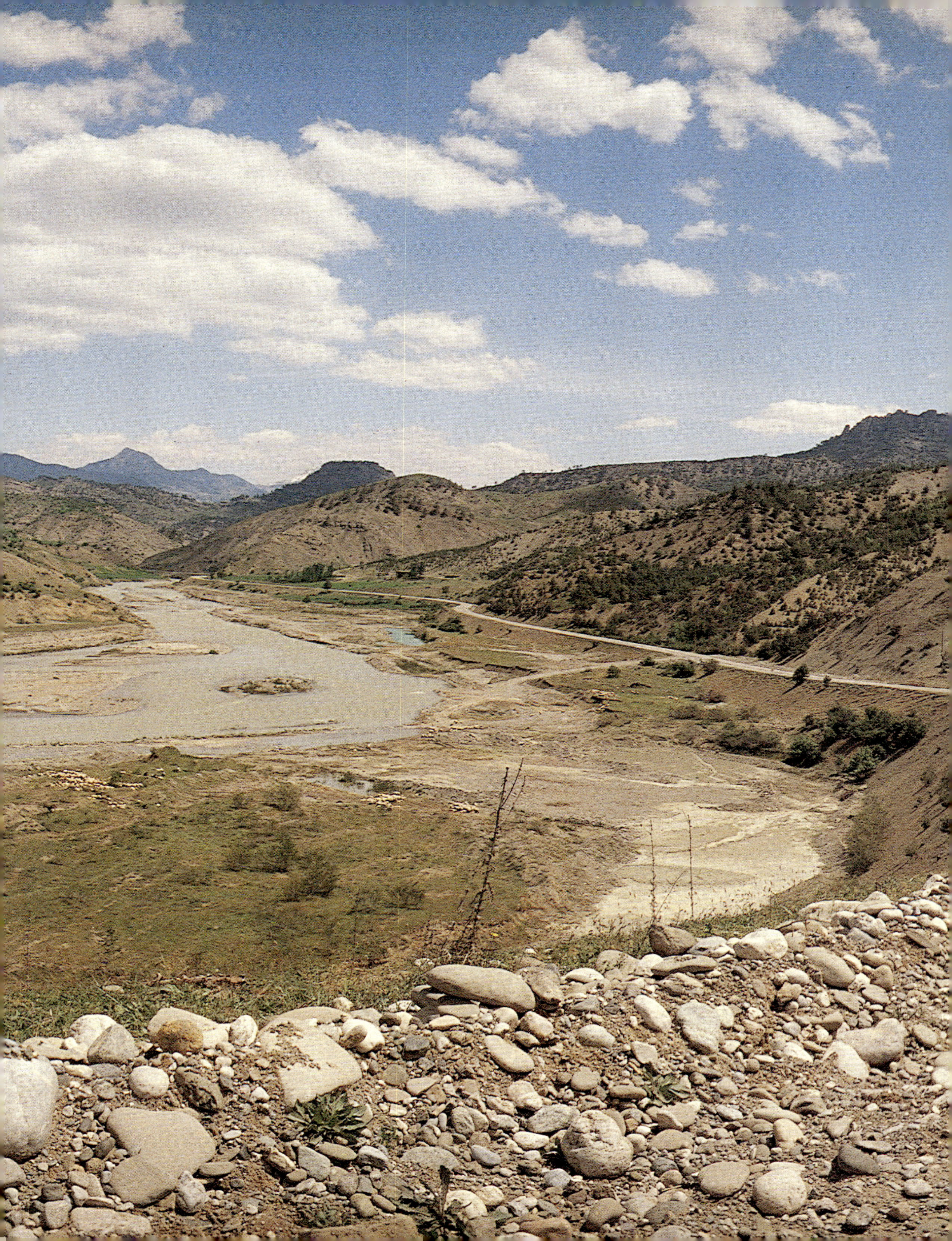

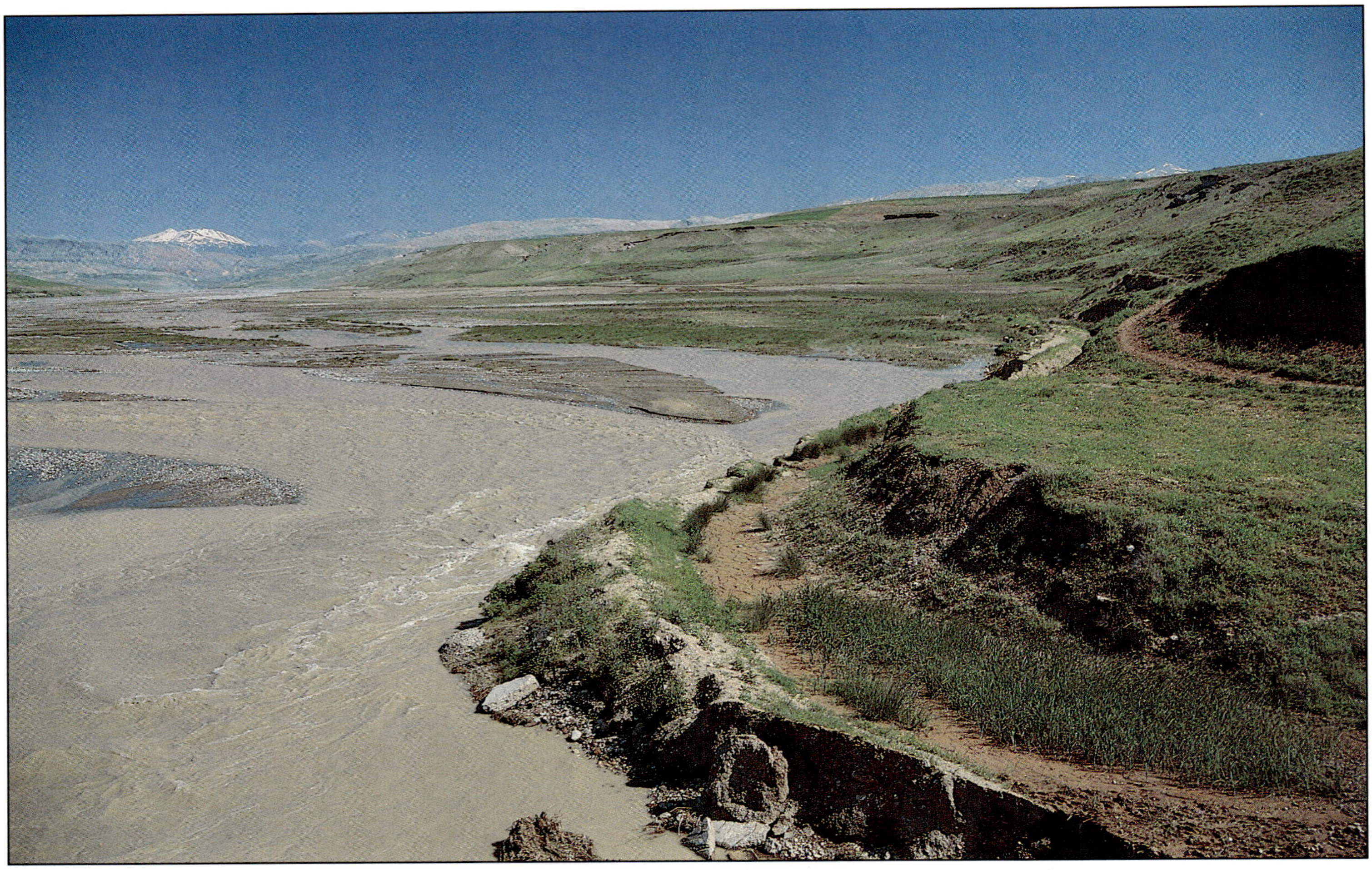

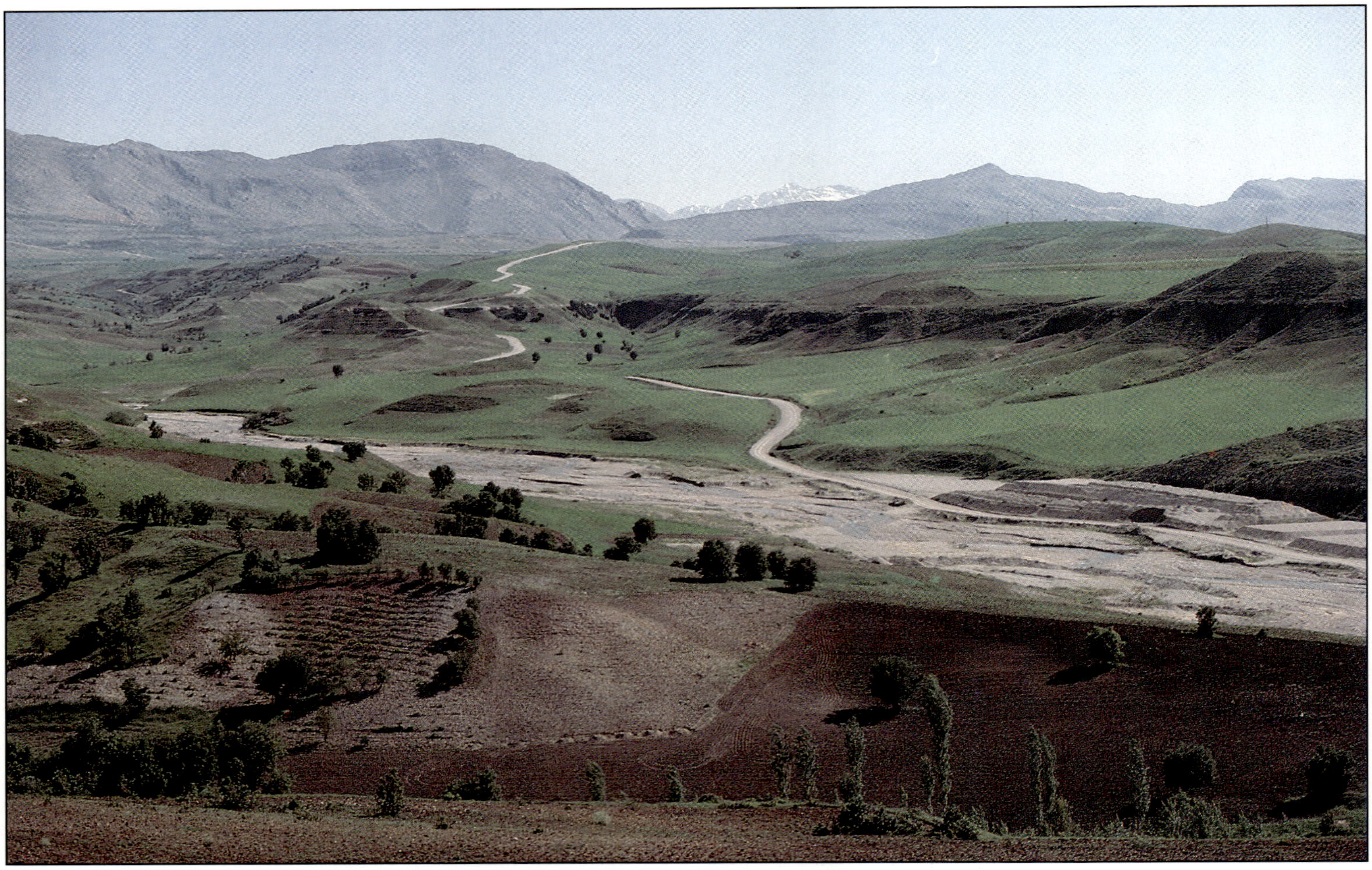

Facing page: the Euphrates River at the foot of Nemrut Dağ in central Turkey. This magnificent river begins in the Turkish highlands, reaching the sea some 2,100 miles later. The region between the Euphrates and the Tigris rivers was in ancient times elaborately irrigated and very fertile. Modern irrigation schemes have yet to equal the achievements of those times, but good grazing (overleaf) still exists on the plain between these rivers. Above left and below: the Tahtalı range in Cappadocia, and (right) an Ottoman bridge over the Ceyhan River west of Kahramanmaras. Above: volcanic tuff between Avanos and Ürgüp in Cappadocia, and (below right) below Nemrut Dağ.

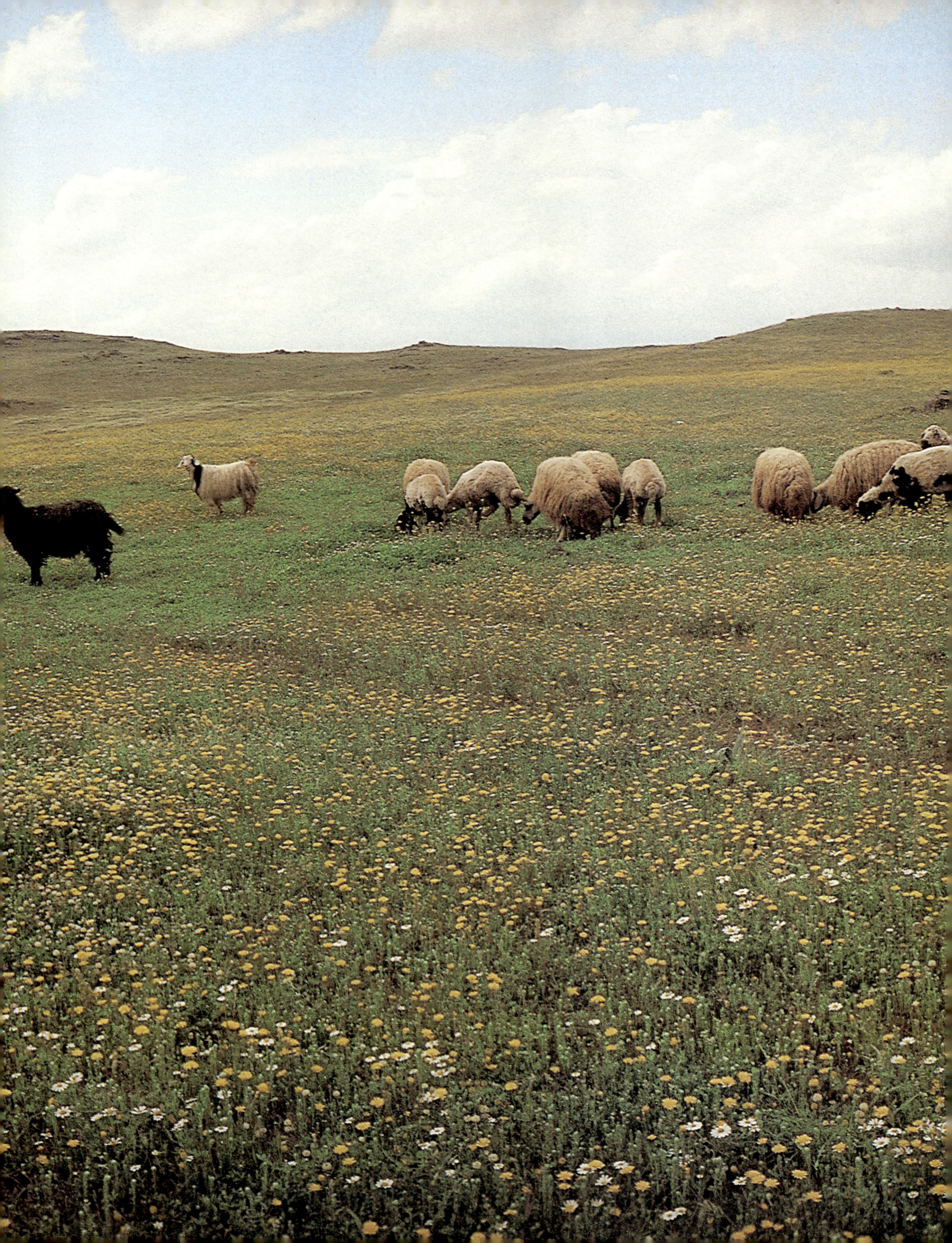

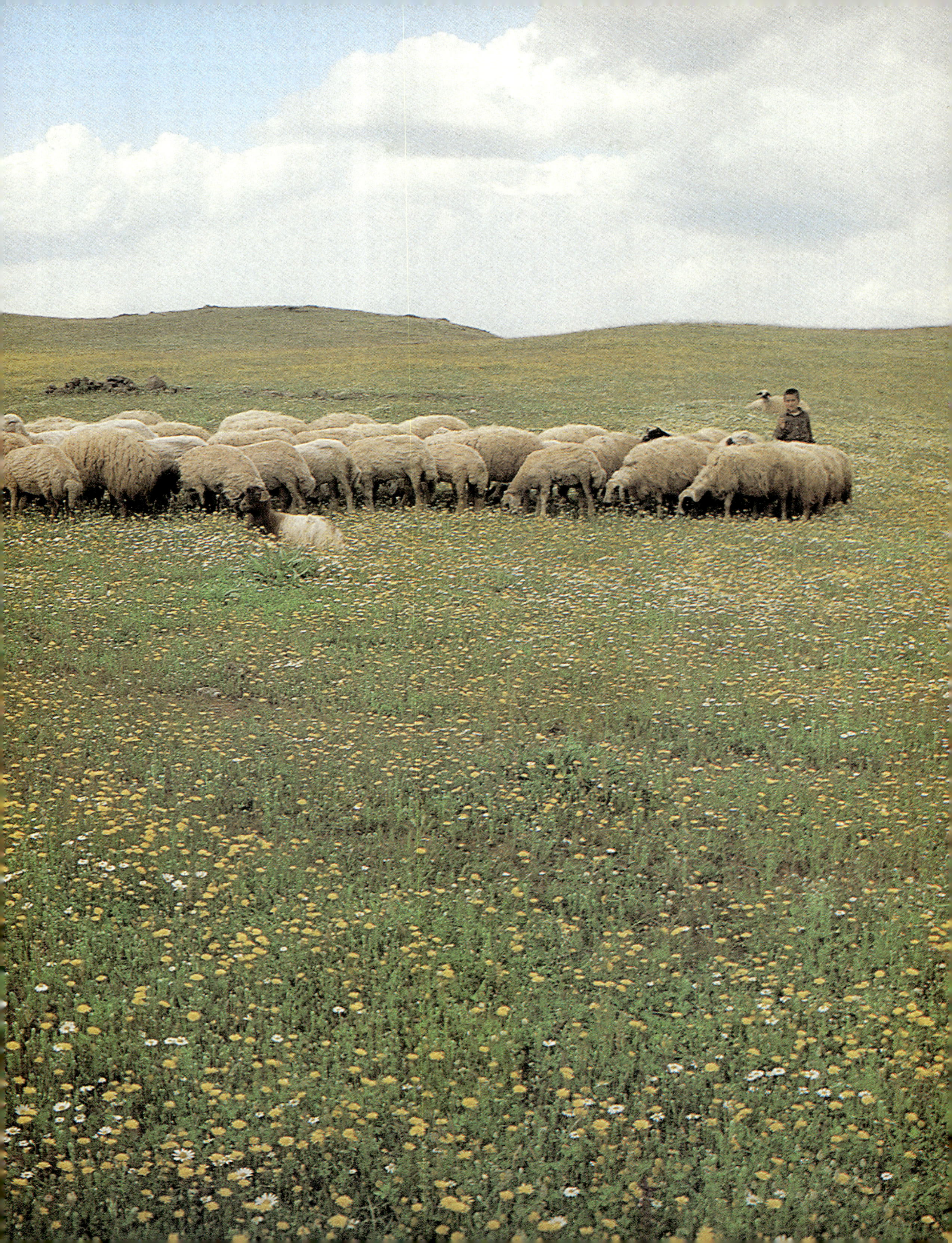

Left: sacks of seeds and spices, (above left) cherries, a fruit which was first cultivated in Turkey, and (below left) beads – produce typical of a Turkish bazaar such as that in Avanos (above). Below: a rug weaver in an Avanos carpet shop; carpets in Turkey range from handmade silk items that can cost thousands to simply colored cotton rugs that the Turks use around the house. Facing page top: Kayseri, a town in Cappadocia founded by the Romans. The latter named it Caesarea in honor of the emperor Caesar Augustus. Facing page bottom: the tunneled rock of Ürçhisar, which lies in the center of the Cappadocian village of the same name.

19

Tufa is a stone comprised of compressed volcanic ash. It is very common in Cappadocia (these pages) in southwestern Anatolia, where three large volcanoes have erupted. Since it is a soft material, tufa is susceptible to erosion – and is easy to carve and tunnel. As a consequence, the weirdest rock formations have been created, such as those in Urçhisar (overleaf). Many of these have been hollowed out to become residences. The region was particularly attractive to early Christians – this was a center of Christian monasticism for several centuries and numerous rock paintings here bear witness to those times. Below: Çavusin, an ancient rock village, and (below right) an example of the rock towers known as fairy chimneys that are common in this region. Bottom right: the open-air museum at Zelve. This village has been carved into the rock and the churches and mosques within it indicate that during one period the Christians and Moslems lived here together. Zelve was used as a hiding place for monks when, during the later days of the Byzantine Empire, anti-Christian Turkish tribes raided the region.

21

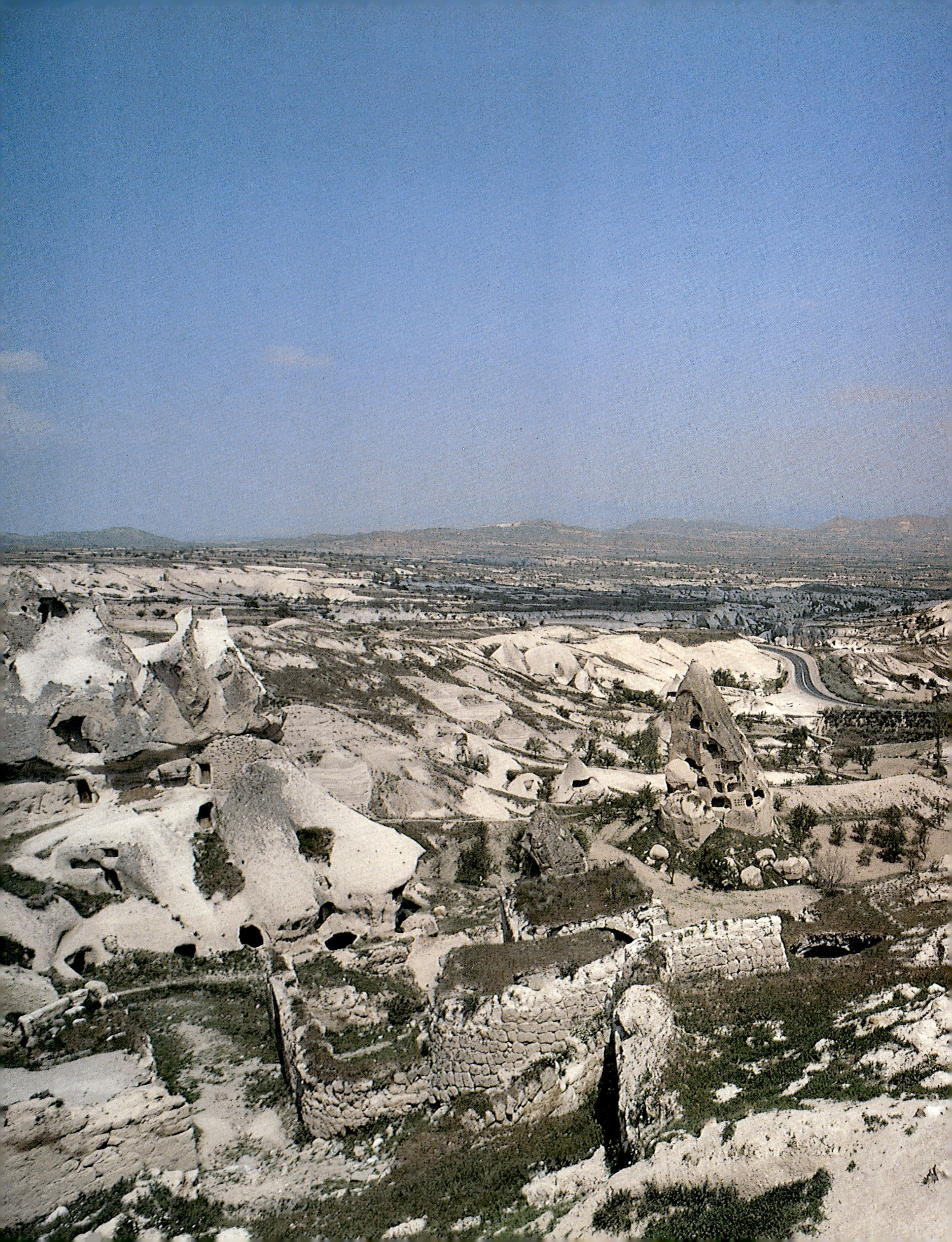

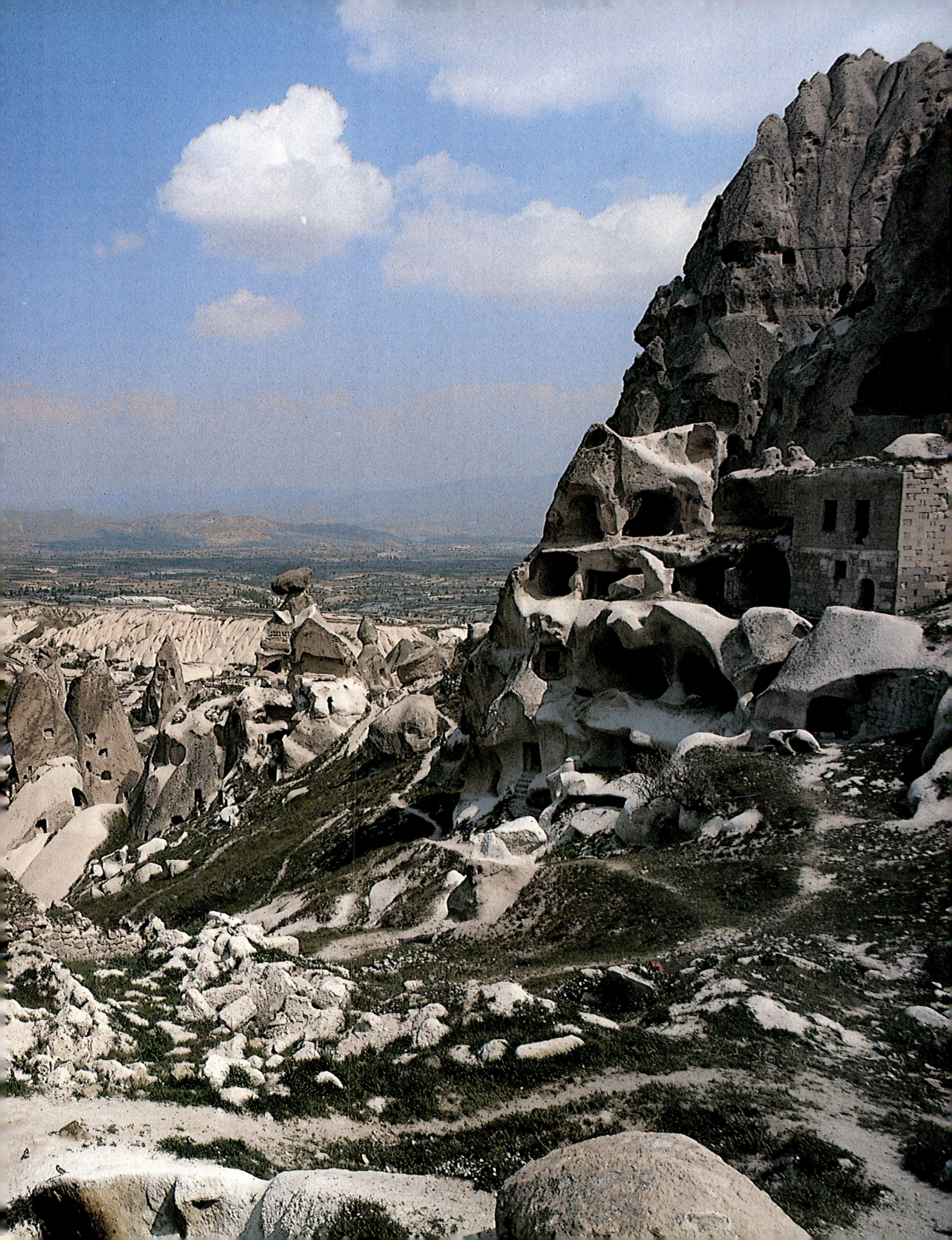

Below: the cave church at Göreme in Cappadocia known as the Dark Church. Restored by UNESCO, the frescoes in this church are some of the best in Cappadocia. Facing page: the Apple Church, Göreme: churches here are identified by some feature of the paintings on their walls.

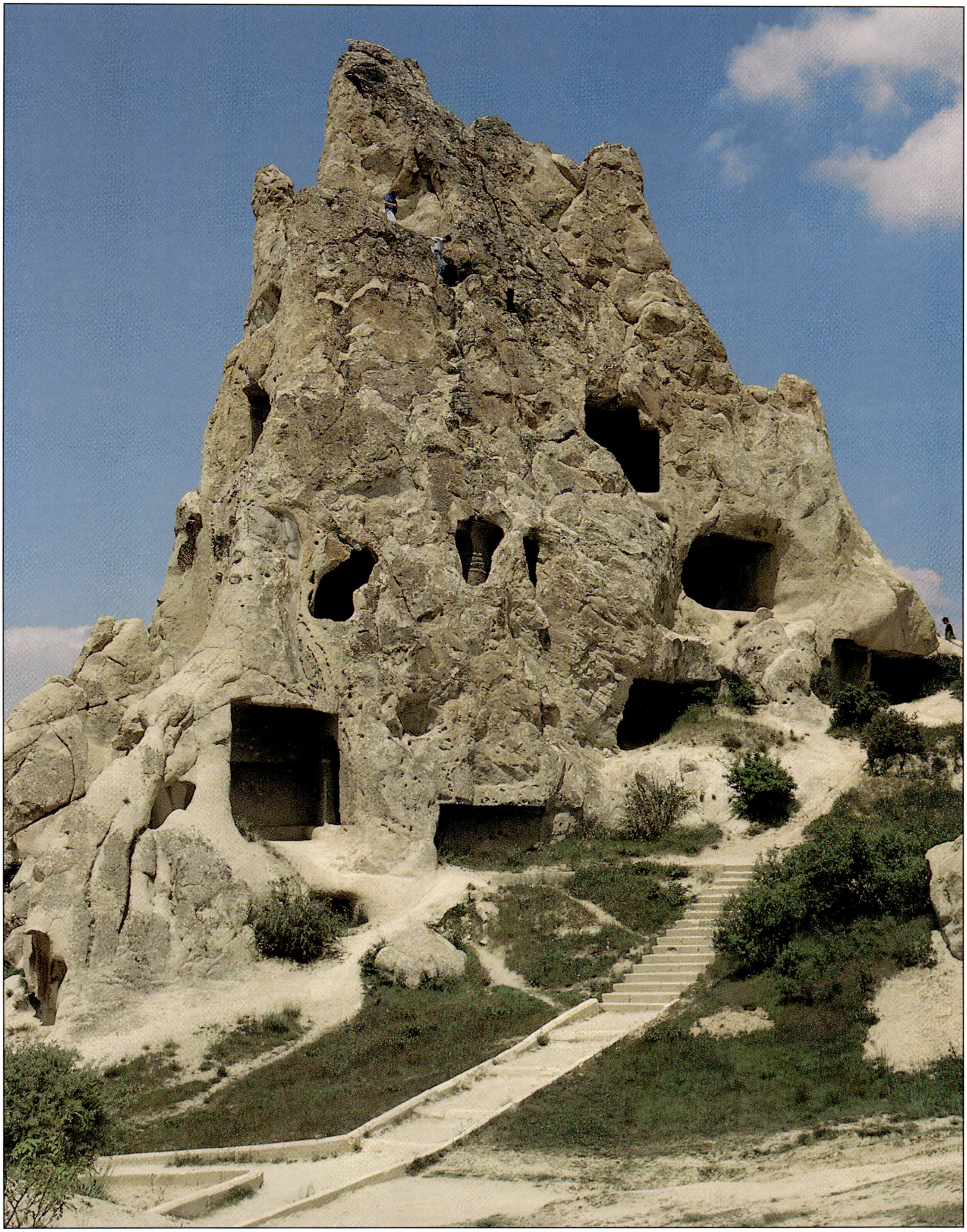

26

One of the best known sites in Cappadocia (below) is the Göreme open-air museum (below left), which encompasses over two dozen churches – the largest monastic complex in the region. The valley that contains them is an extensive one – visitors can spend days exploring the stairs, paths and tunnels that connect the churches. The paintings on the walls within them fall into two distinct categories: those painted during the eighth and ninth centuries, which are primitive, and those of the tenth century, which are among the finest Byzantine works ever created. Bottom left: the underground city of Özkonak, the most recently opened and the largest of these in Cappadocia. Özkonak is an elaborate network of tunnels, some over six miles long, stairways and chambers hollowed out of the rock. Air shafts provide ventilation and underground wells drinking water. Incredibly, in times of trouble, when the land was invaded by hostile armies, up to 20,000 people were able to live here, the entrances being sealed by massive rolling stones. Left and overleaf: fairy chimneys in the valleys of Zelve, which lie northeast of Göreme.

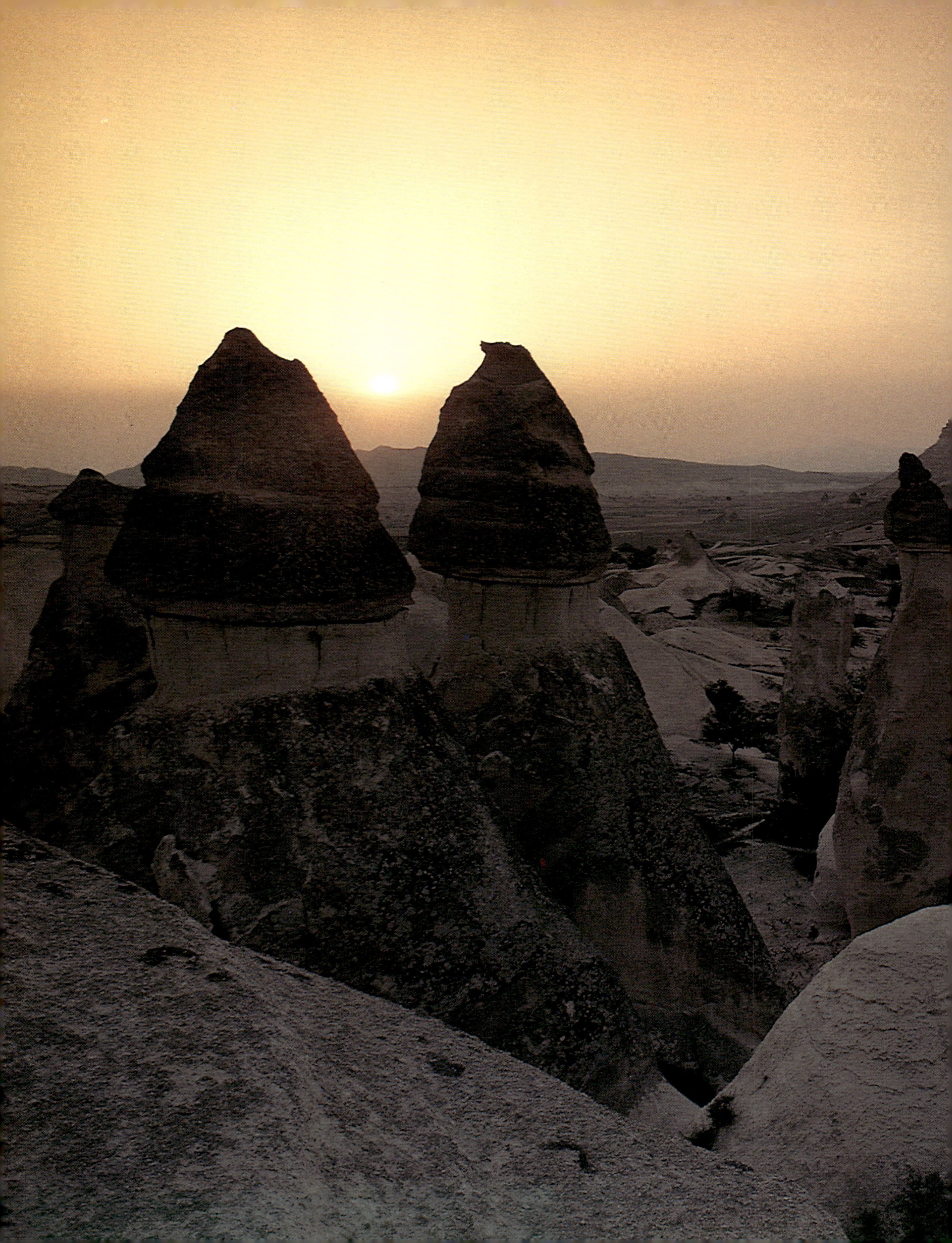

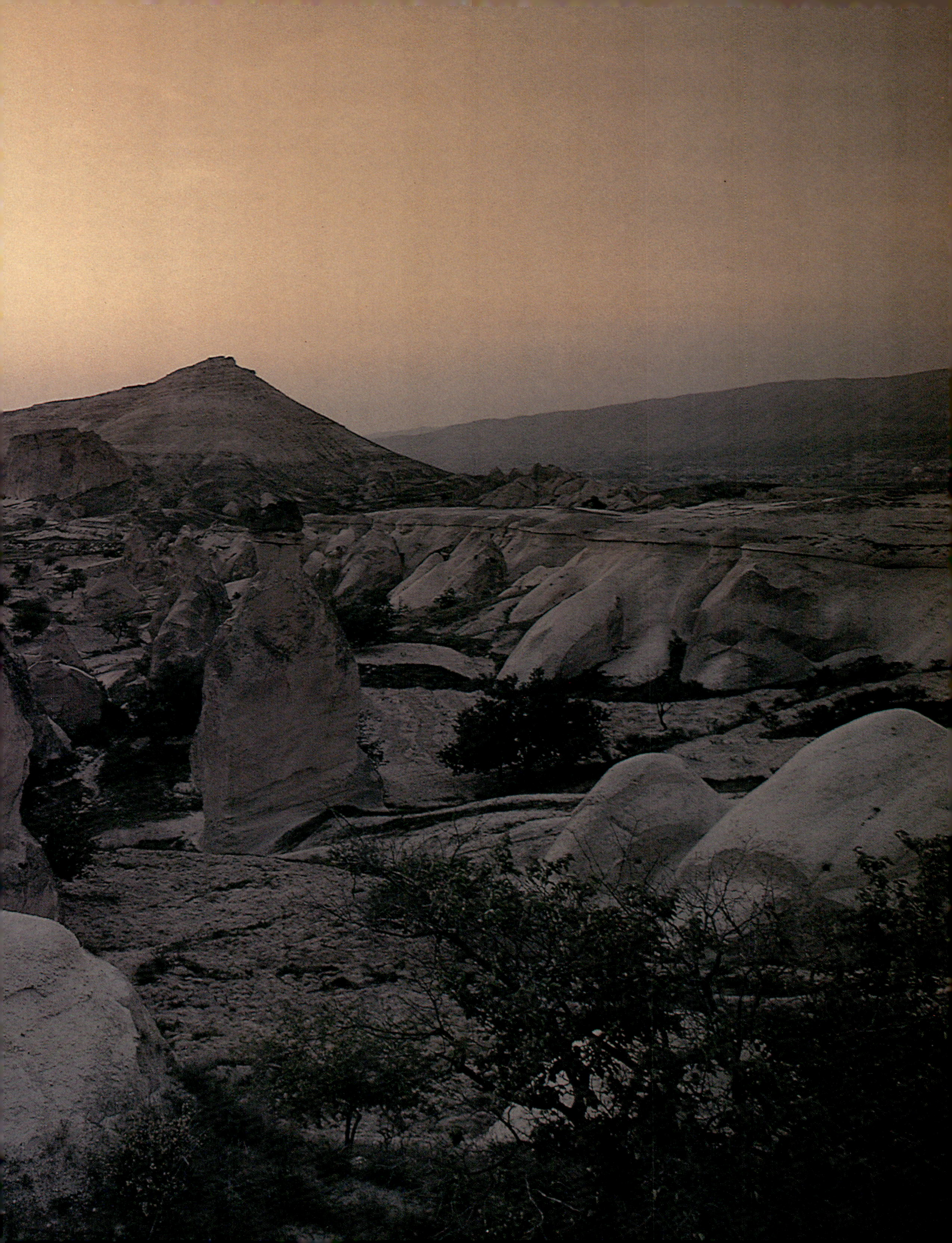

Below and right: Atatürk's Mausoleum, known as Anıt Kabir, in Ankara, the capital of Turkey. Kemal Atatürk was the Turkish leader who helped defeat the British at Gallipoli in 1915 during the First World War and who was responsible for westernizing the country. His surname means "father of the Turks" and, as such, he is still considered with reverential awe by his countrymen, though he died in 1938. It was his decision that Turkey's new capital should be more central than Istanbul had been – Ankara lies nearer the heart of Turkey, though not in the geographical center. The mausoleum grounds cover a large area in the middle of Ankara; at their center is the monumental limestone building which shelters the colossal stone sarcophagus that is Atatürk's final resting place. On the walls are quotes from the speeches of the great leader. Right: the Sphinx Gate to the ancient city of Hattusas east of Ankara. This was once the capital of the Hittites, a people who, 3,000 years ago, rivaled the Egyptians in the extent of their empire. Indeed, one of the most famous Egyptian pharaohs, Ramses II, married a Hittite king's daughter.

EDİLMİŞ, BÜTÜN TERSANELERİNE GİRİLMİŞ, BÜTÜN ORDULARI
DAĞITILMIŞ VE MEMLEKETİN HER KÖŞESİ BİLFİİL İŞGAL EDİLMİŞ
OLABİLİR. BÜTÜN BU ŞERAİTTEN DAHA ELİM VE DAHA VAHİM
OLMAK ÜZERE, MEMLEKETİN DAHİLİNDE, İKTİDARA SAHİP OLAN-
LAR GAFLET VE DALÂLET VE HATTA HIYANET İÇİNDE BULUNABİ-
LİRLER. HATTA BU İKTİDAR SAHİPLERİ ŞAHSİ MENFAATLERİNİ
MÜSTEVLİLERİN SİYASİ EMELLERİYLE TEVHİT EDEBİLİRLER.
MİLLET, FAKRÜ ZARURET İÇİNDE HARAP VE BİTAP DÜŞMÜŞ
OLABİLİR.
EY TÜRK İSTİKBALİNİN EVLADI !
İŞTE BU AHVAL VE ŞERAİT İÇİNDE DAHİ VAZİFEN, TÜRK
İSTİKLALİNİ VE TÜRK CUMHURİYETİNİ KURTARMAKTIR.
MUHTAÇ OLDUĞUN KUDRET
MEVCUTTUR !

Istanbul (these pages), formerly known as Constantinople, and before that as Byzantium, is the only city on earth to stand on two continents. It is Turkey's largest metropolis and one of the oldest cities in the world. Above: the ceiling of the Blue Mosque, which dates from 1619 and is lined with over 20,000 blue tiles; these have given the mosque its name. Below left and facing page: Süleymaniye Mosque, thought to be the zenith of Ottoman art, and (left) the Haghia Sophia Museum, once a magnificent church. Below: the Topkapı Dagger in the Sultans' Treasury, and (above left and overleaf) the European Fortress.

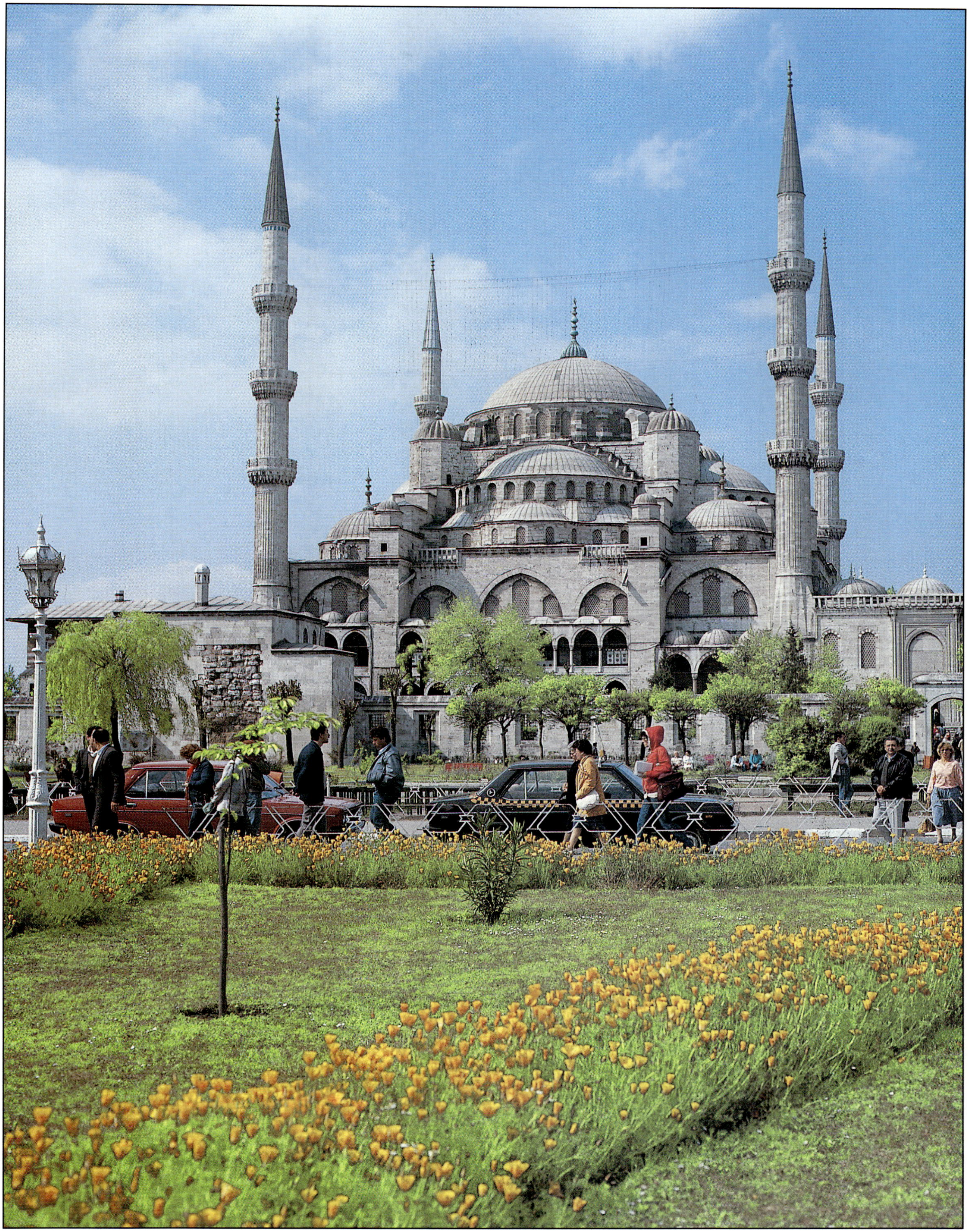

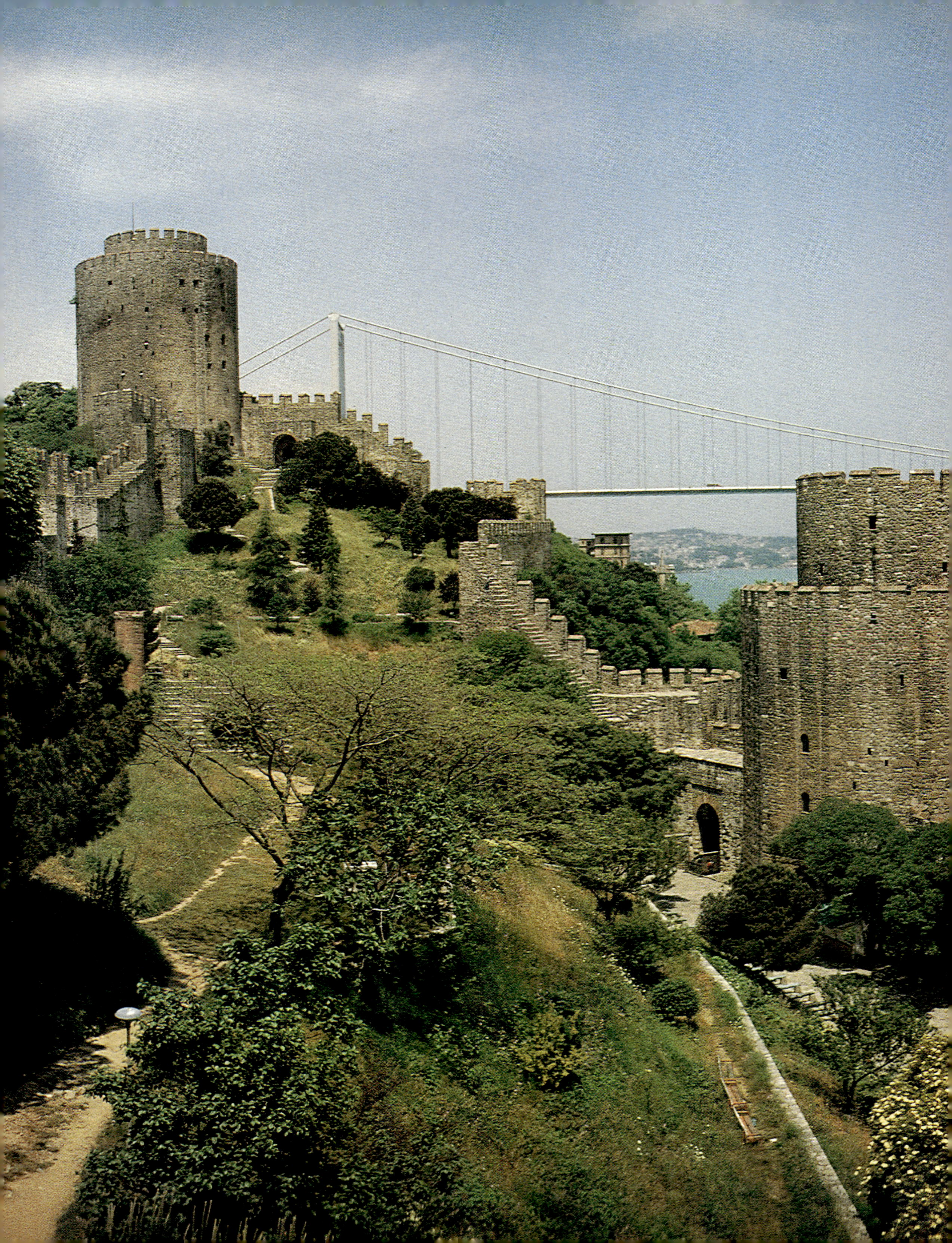

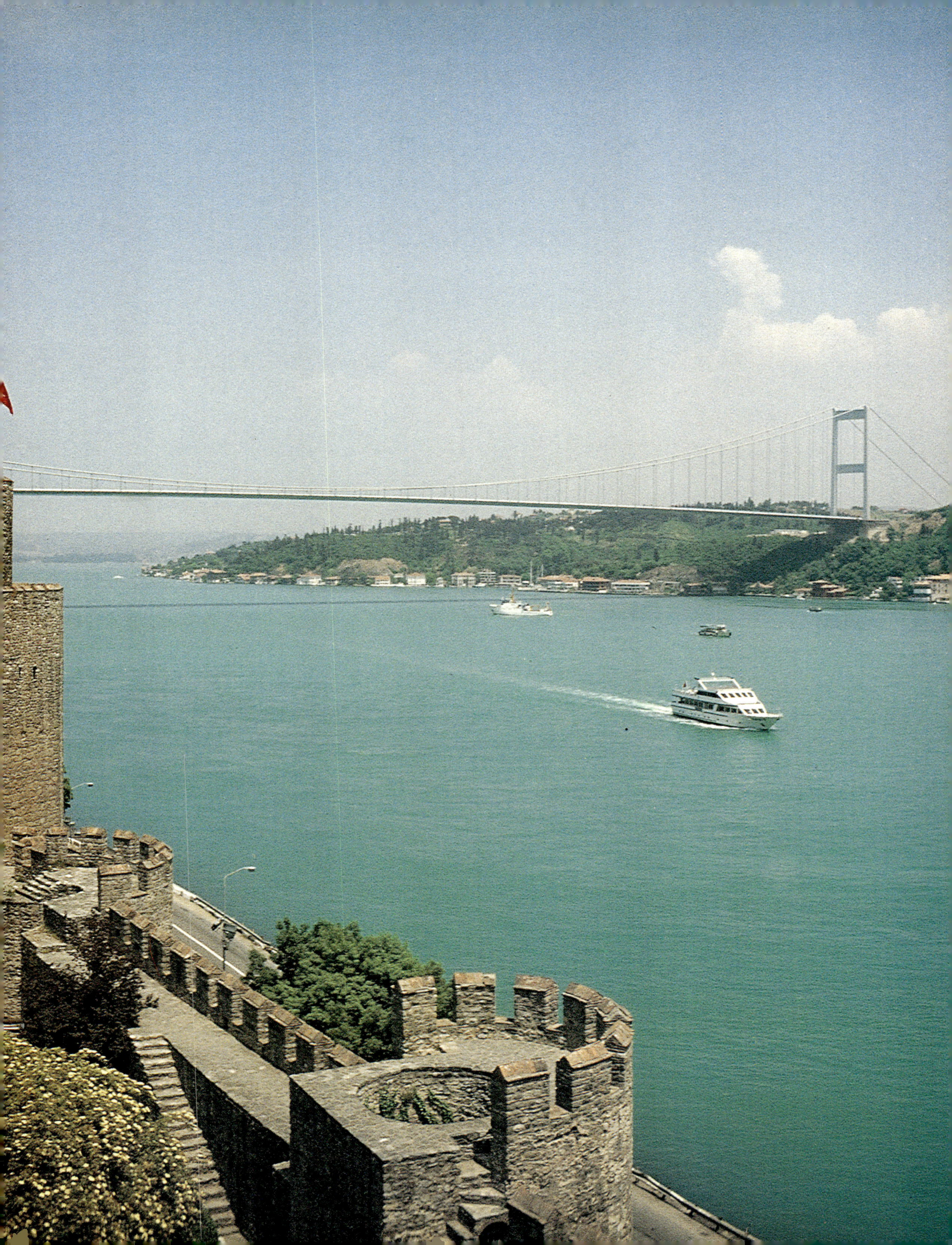

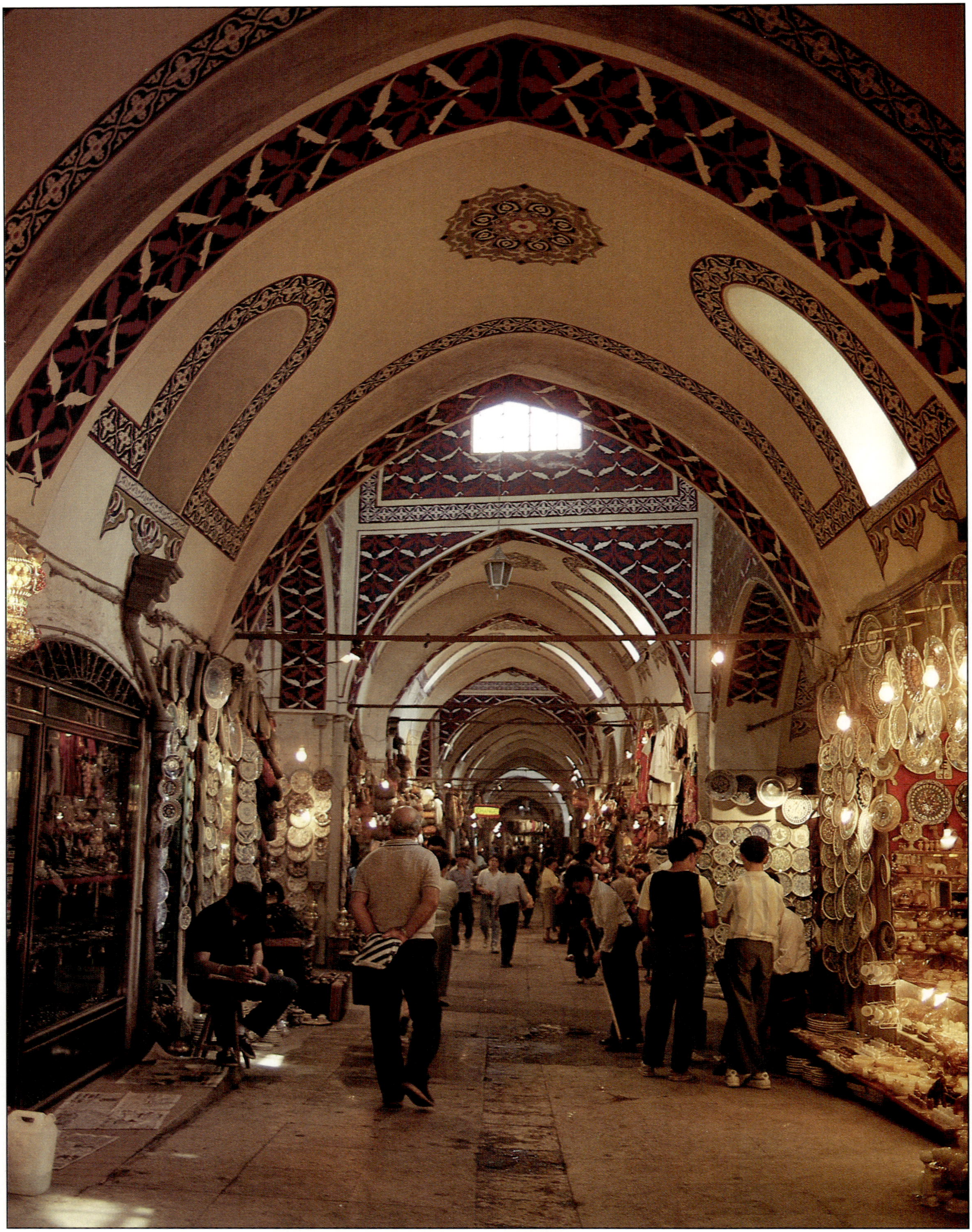

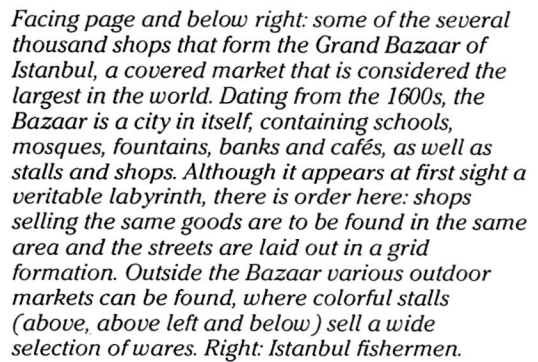

Facing page and below right: some of the several thousand shops that form the Grand Bazaar of Istanbul, a covered market that is considered the largest in the world. Dating from the 1600s, the Bazaar is a city in itself, containing schools, mosques, fountains, banks and cafés, as well as stalls and shops. Although it appears at first sight a veritable labyrinth, there is order here: shops selling the same goods are to be found in the same area and the streets are laid out in a grid formation. Outside the Bazaar various outdoor markets can be found, where colorful stalls (above, above left and below) sell a wide selection of wares. Right: Istanbul fishermen.

Night in Istanbul (these pages) offers another view of the city's great mosques, most of which are floodlit. This great city, the center of the Eastern Mediterranean for sixteen centuries, is particularly special after dark, when it is not difficult to recall the atmosphere in the tales of the Arabian Nights.

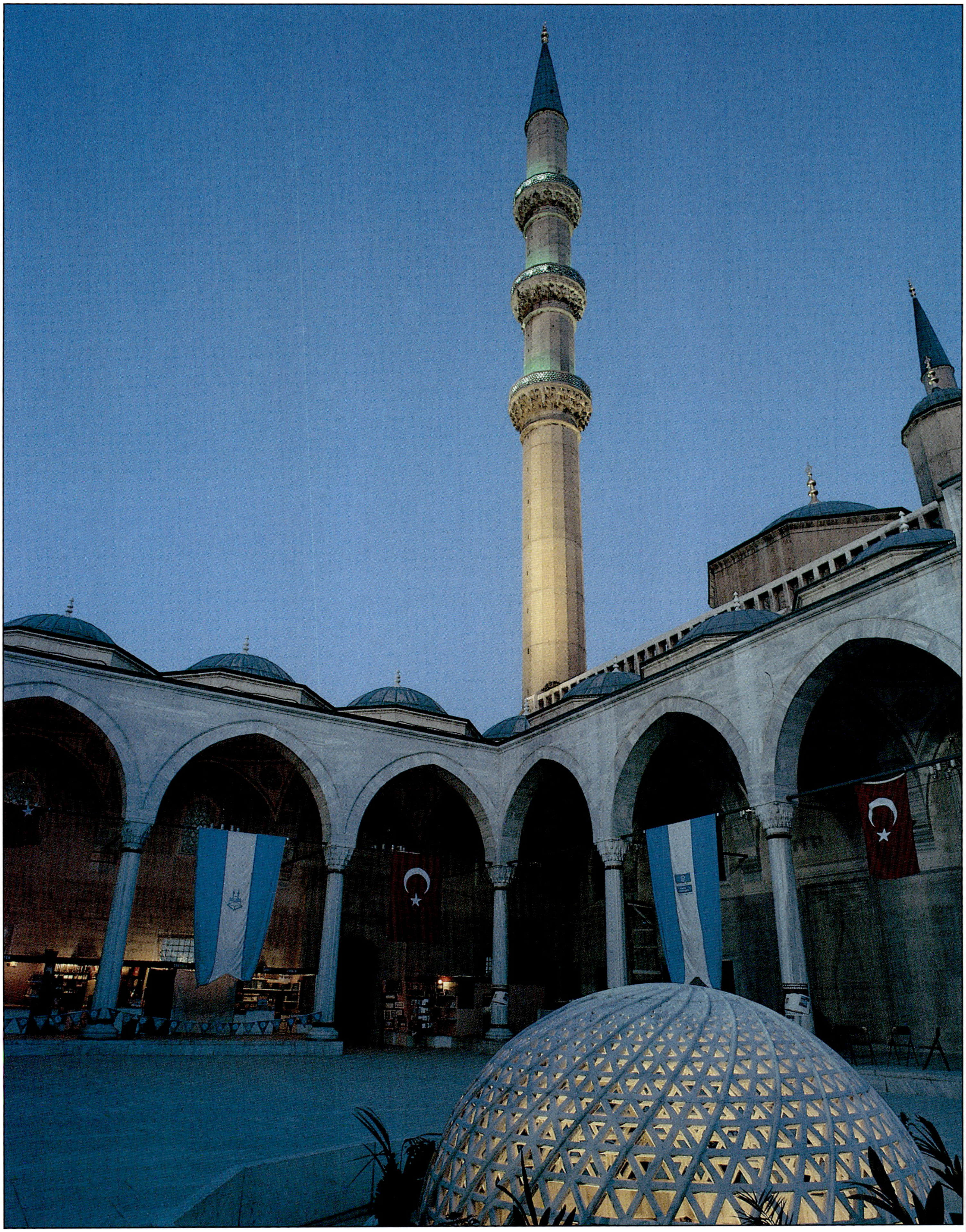

Above, left and below: the Dalmabahçe Palace, Istanbul, a mid-nineteenth century architectural extravaganza where Atatürk died. As a somewhat morbid mark of reverence, all the many clocks of the palace have been stopped at 9.05, the very moment when the great man succumbed. Above left and overleaf: Galata Bridge crosses the Golden Horn, the slender stretch of water that separates the two European sections of Istanbul. Below left: Taksim Square, around which are clustered most of Istanbul's international hotels. Facing page top: the Topkapı Palace from the Bosphorus. The palace, which is thought to be the oldest and largest on earth, has been a museum since 1924.

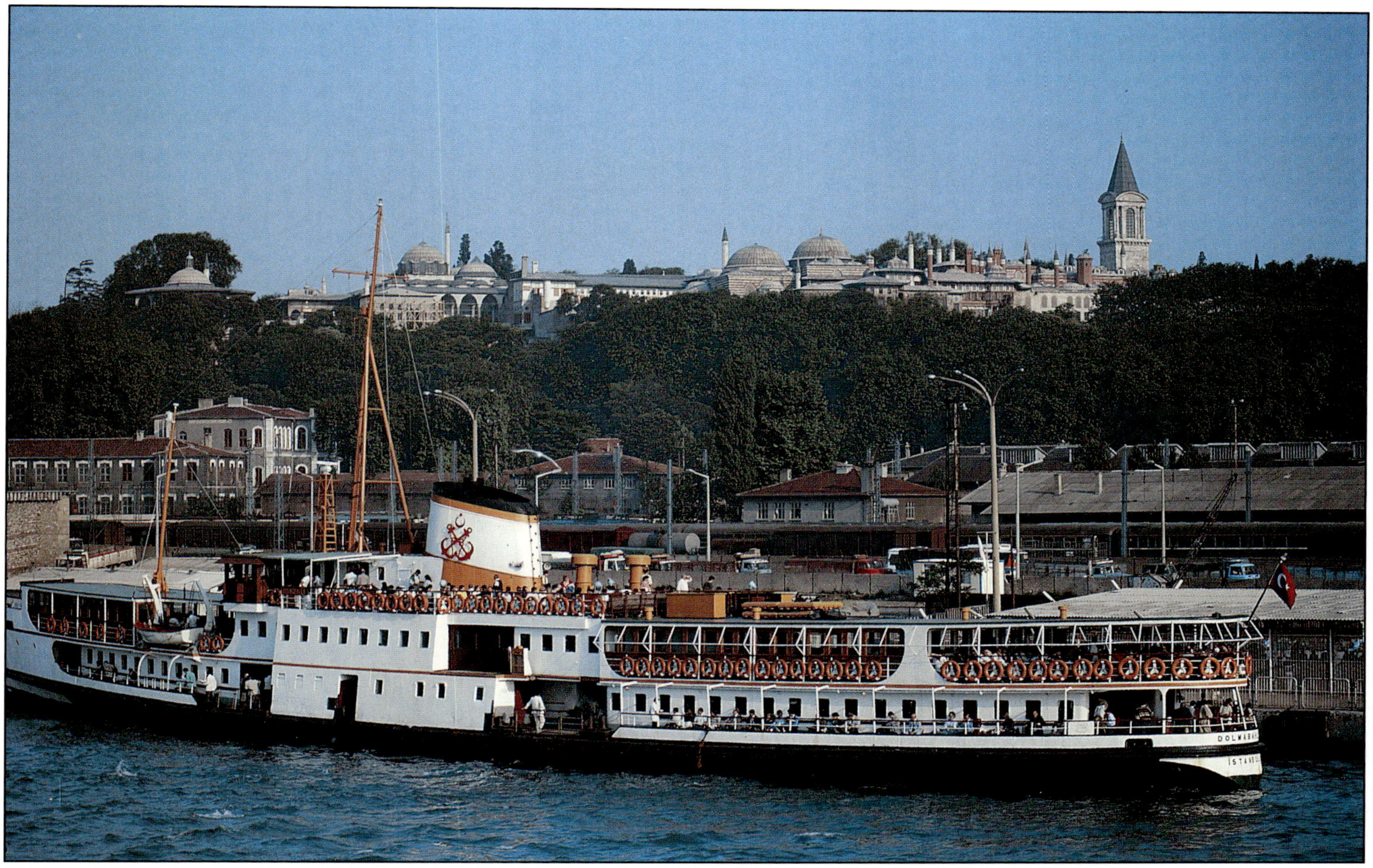

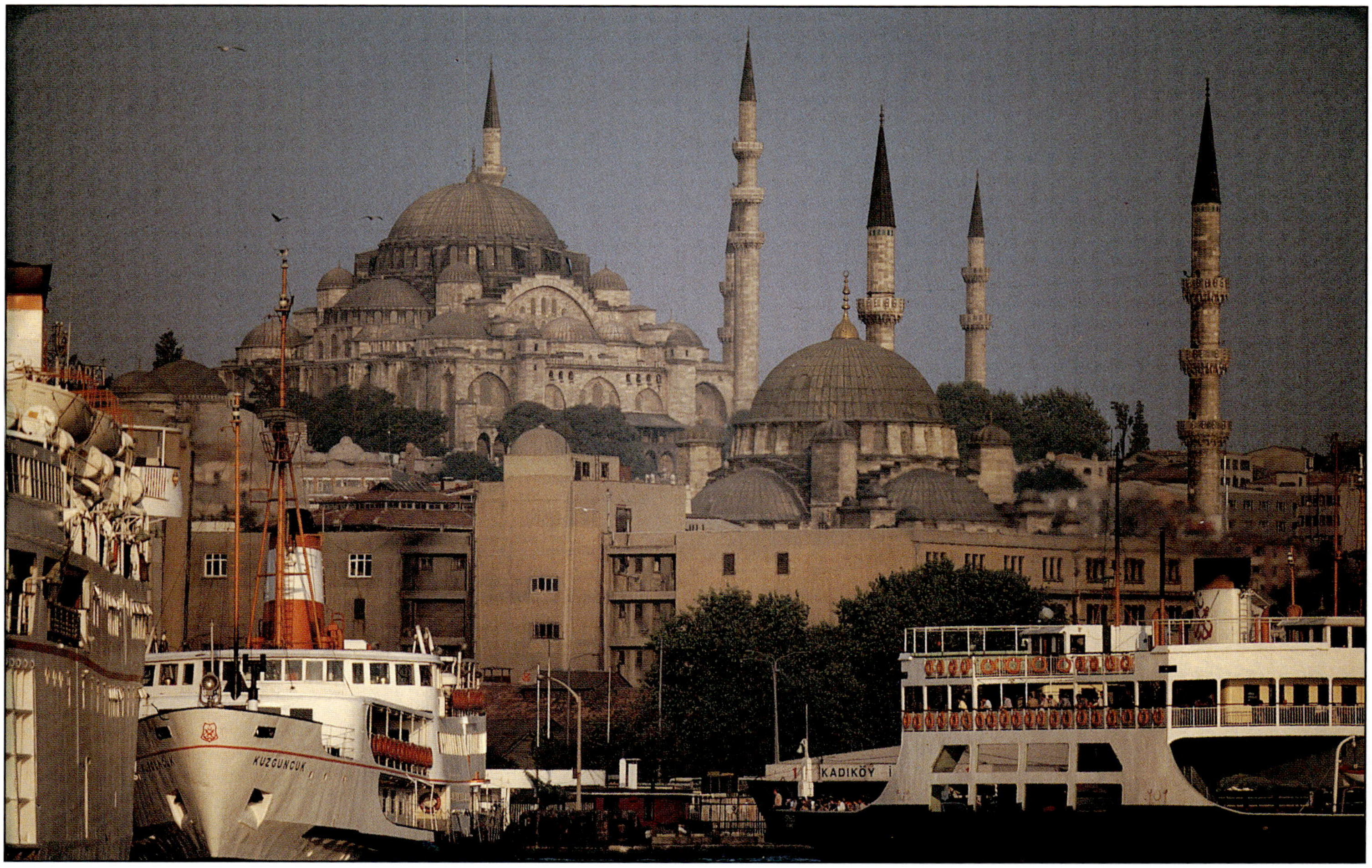
KUZGUNCUK
KADIKÖY

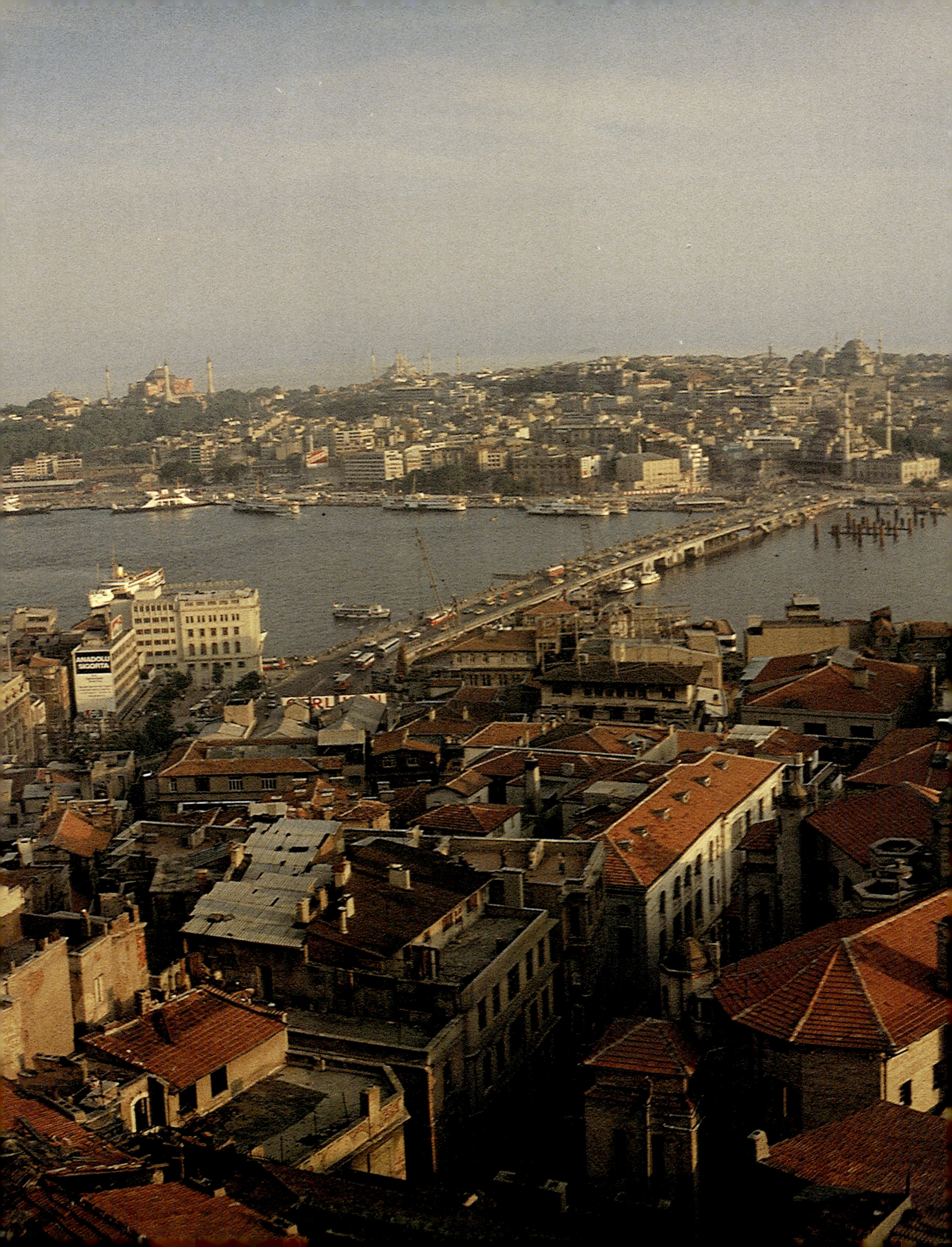
ANADOLU
SIGORTA

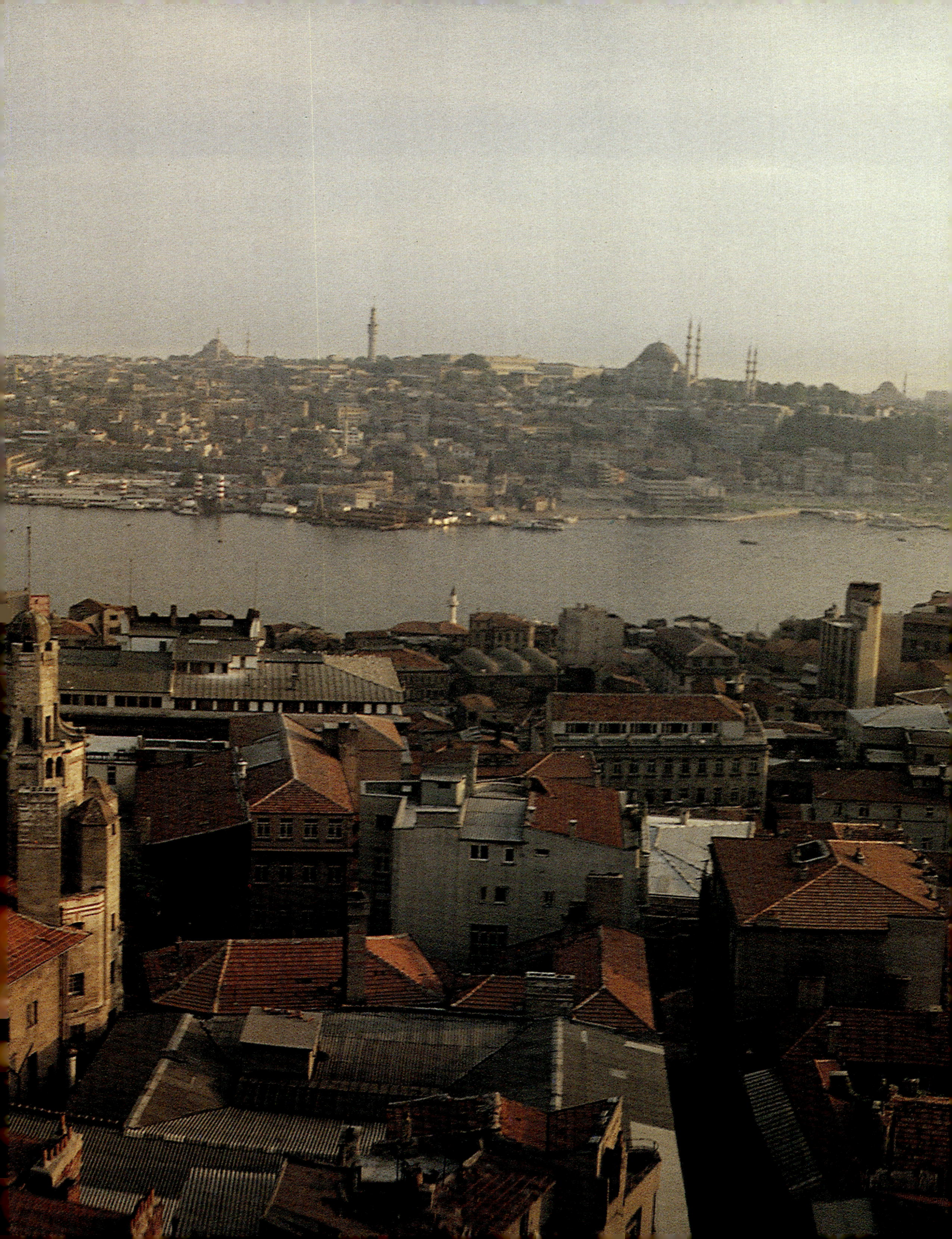

Below: the modern Turkish equivalent of the Wooden Horse of Troy at the site of this ancient, almost mythological city near Çanakkale. Facing page: (top) the ruins of the Temple of Artemis south of Sardis and (bottom) the ruins of a Roman marketplace at Izmir (overleaf).

45

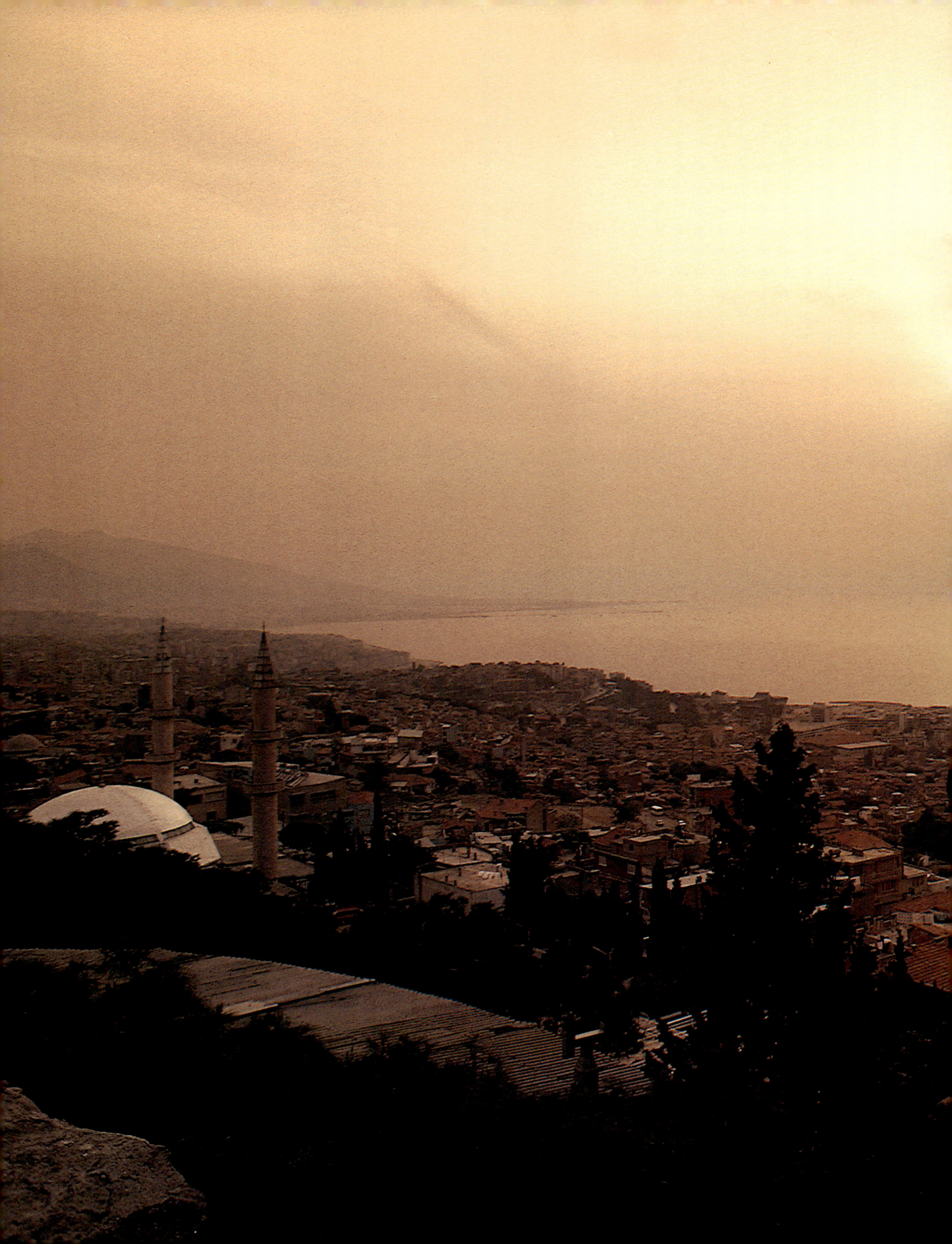

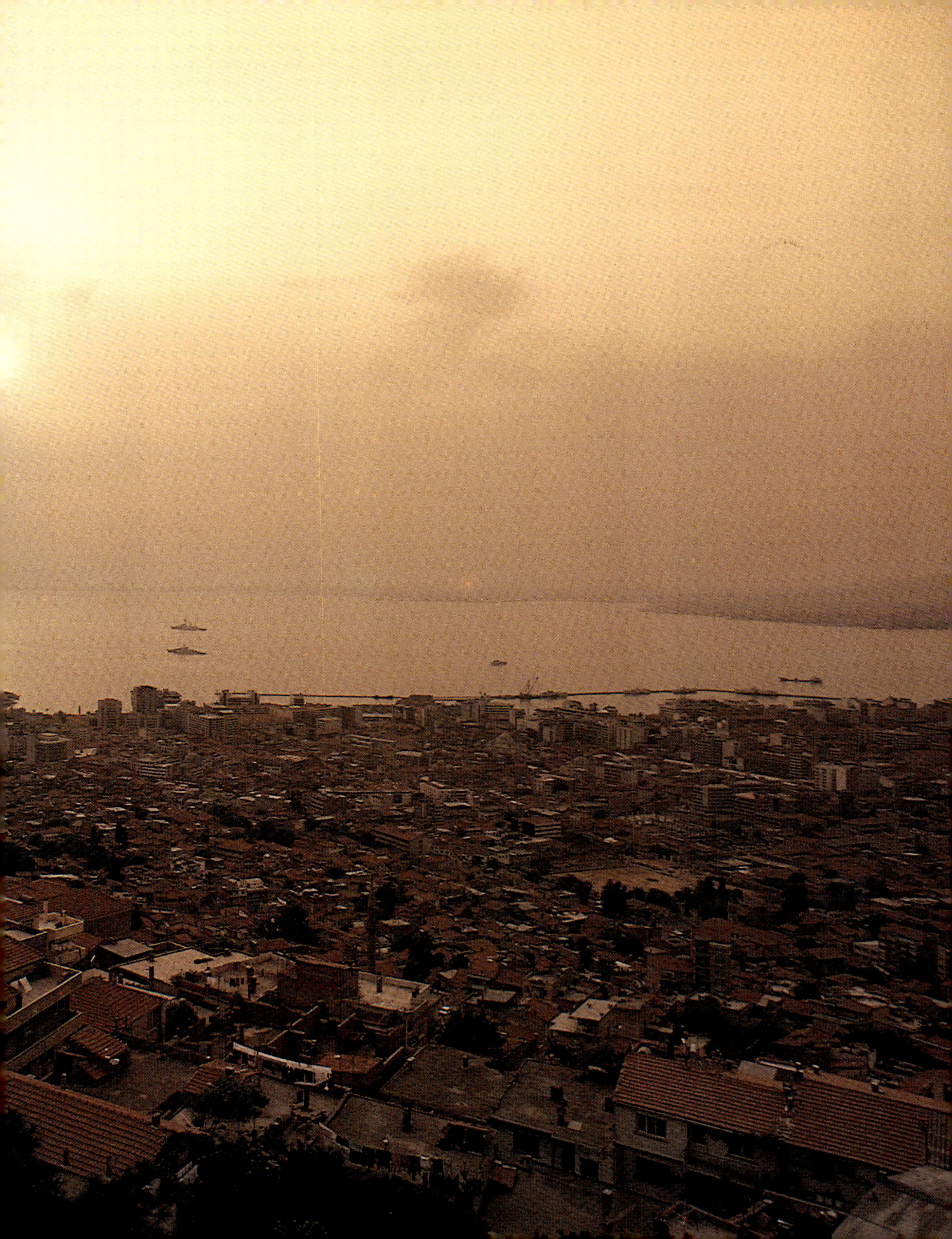

Of all the ancient cities in Turkey, Ephesus (these pages) is the best preserved. Two of the most famous exhibits at Ephesus Museum are the marble head of Eros (above) and an ivory statuette of Artemis (below), a goddess transformed in Ephesus from virgin huntress to earth mother. Left: the Odeon, a small theater once used for lectures and council meetings, (below left) Hadrian's Arch, and (above left) the Hellenistic Great Theater, carved into the side of Mount Pion and remodeled by the Romans. Facing page: (top) the Library of Celsus, considered to be the most elegant of the buildings here, and (bottom) the Arcadiane, the main road to the harbor, built in the fourth century.

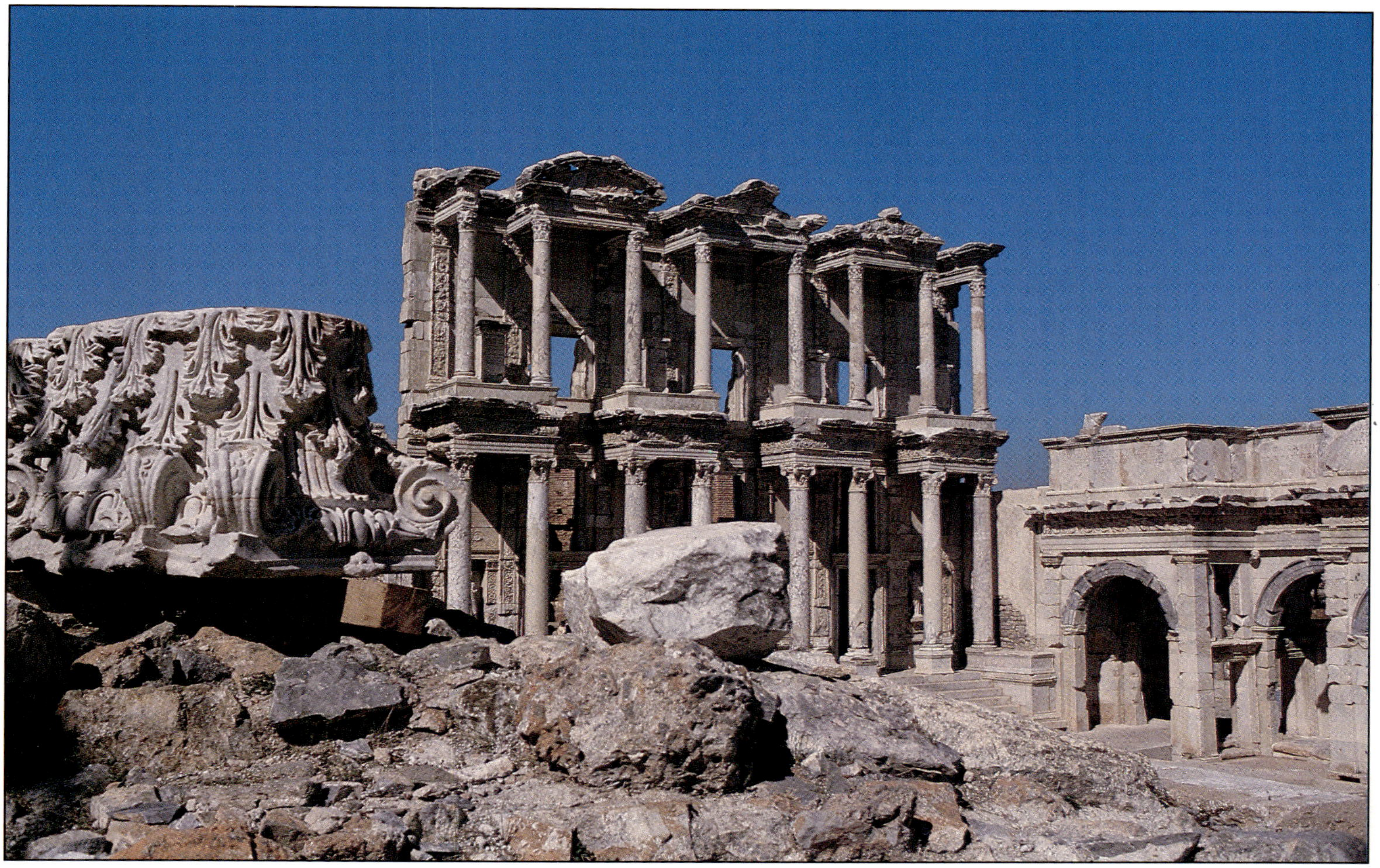

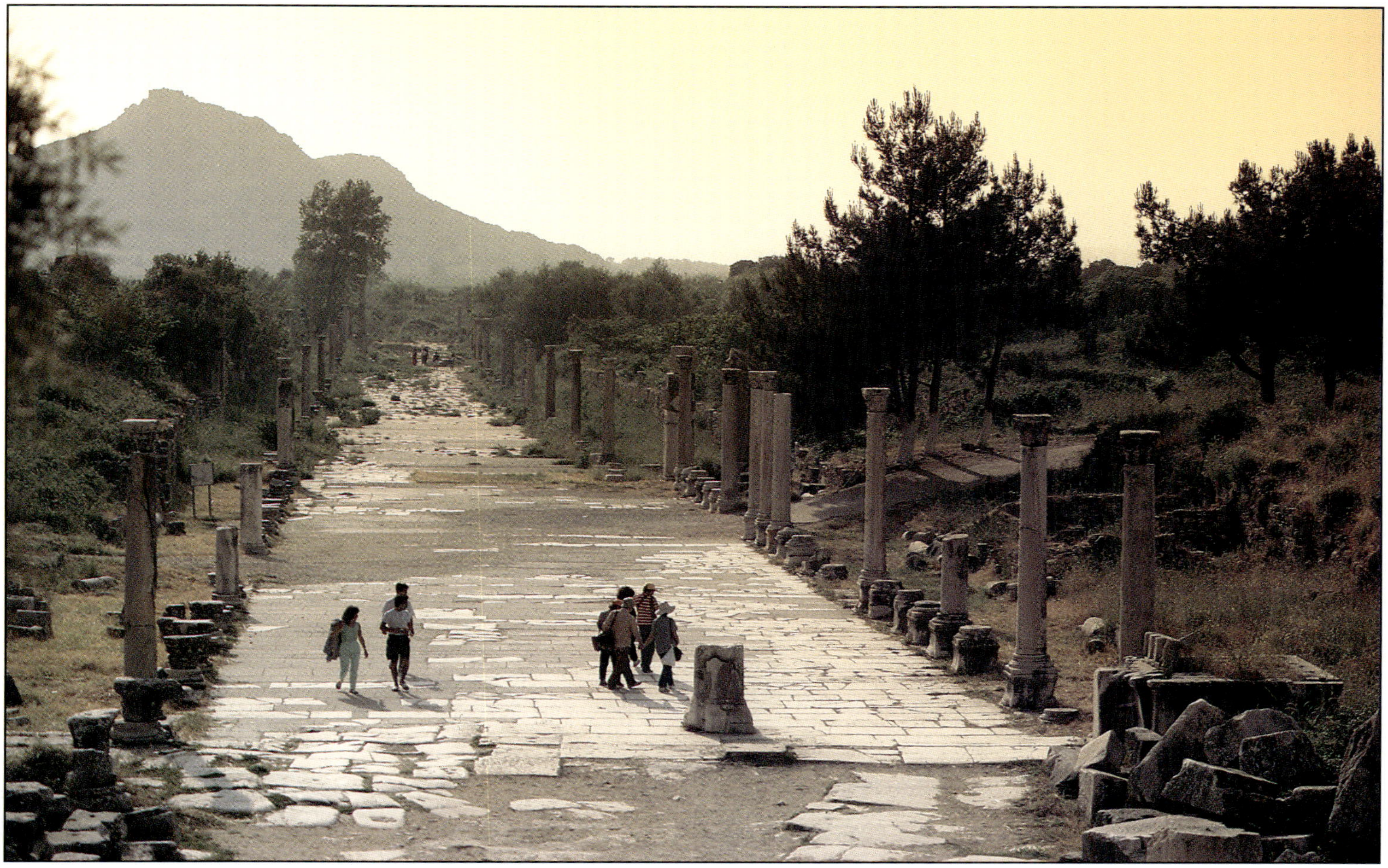

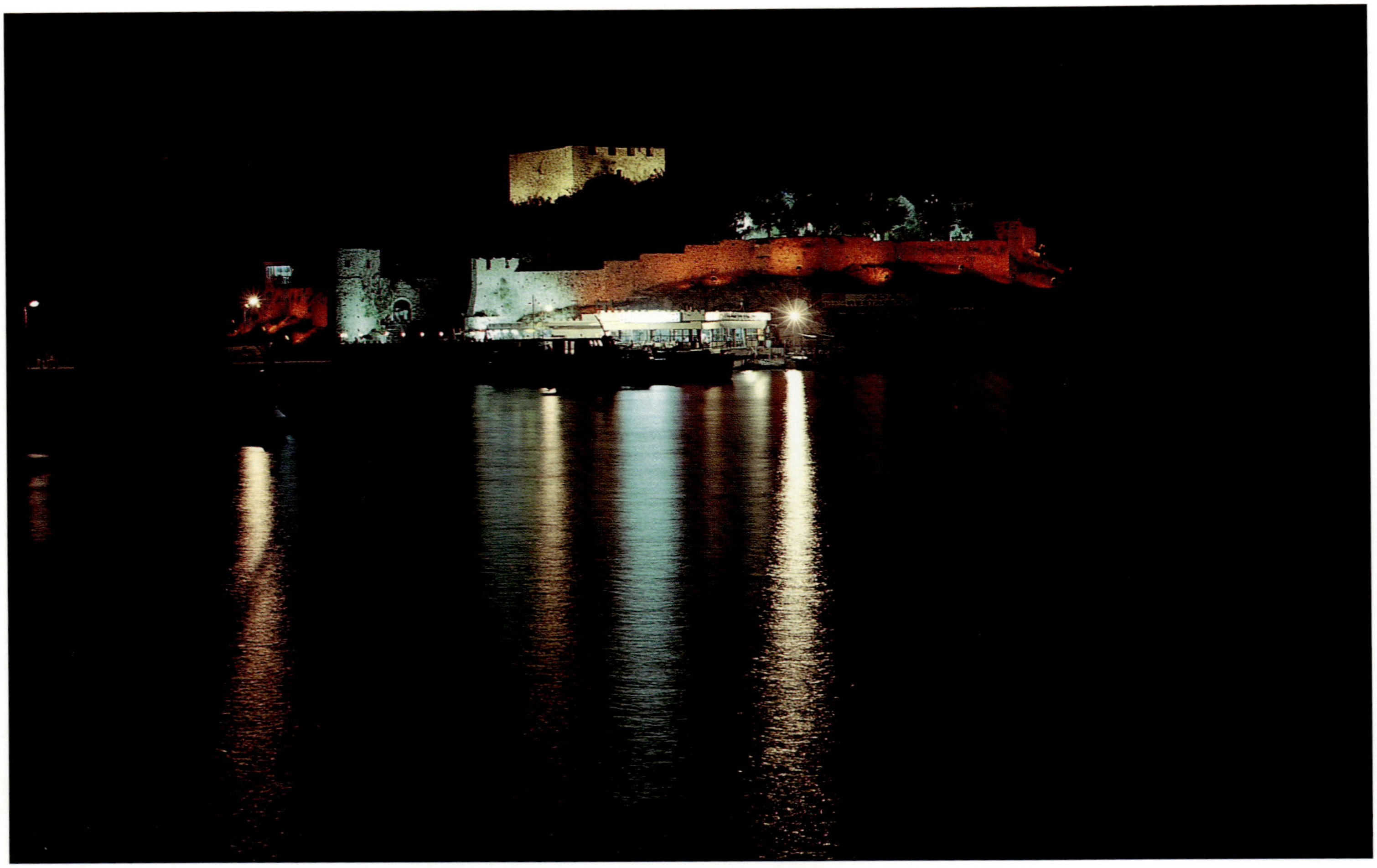

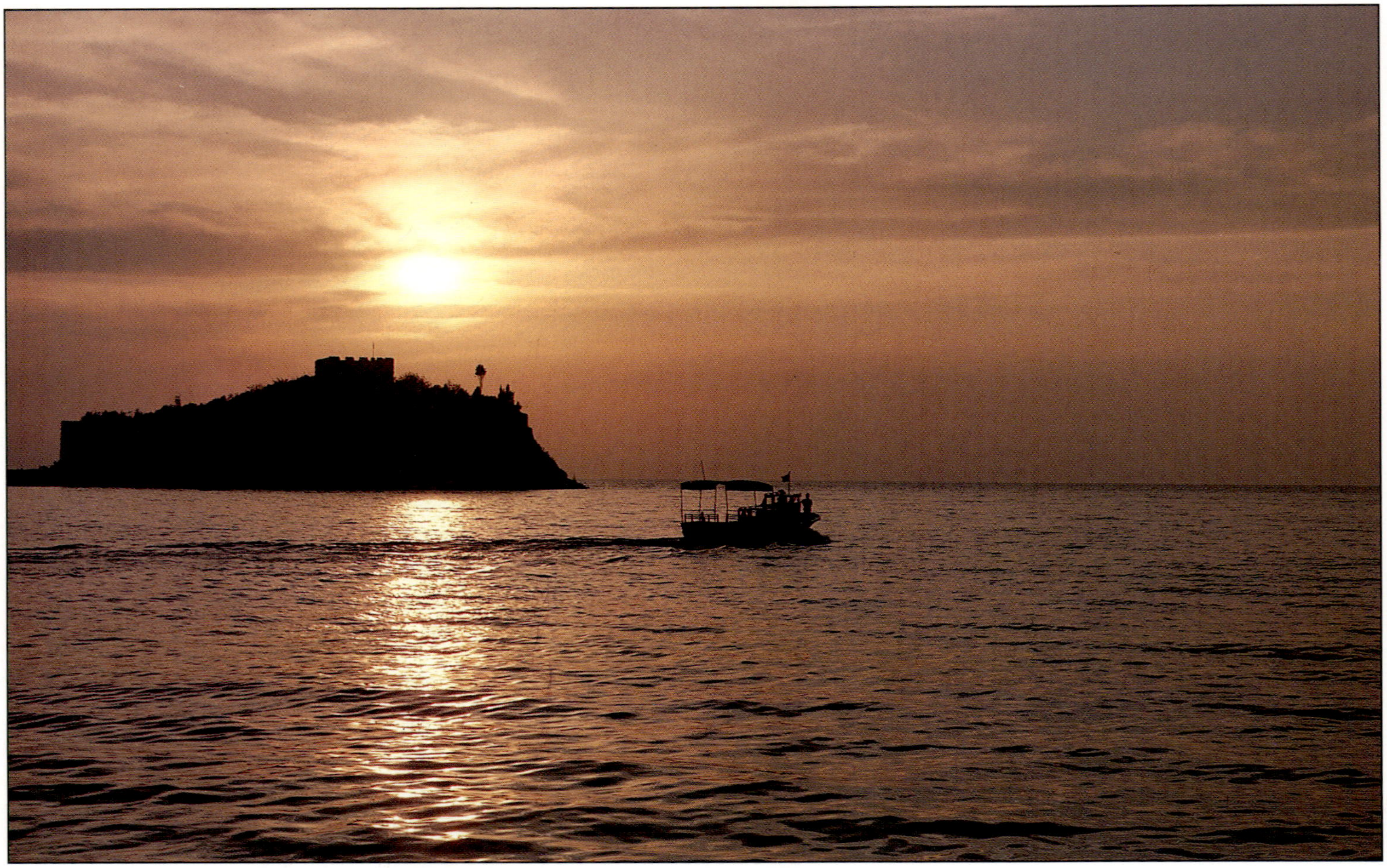

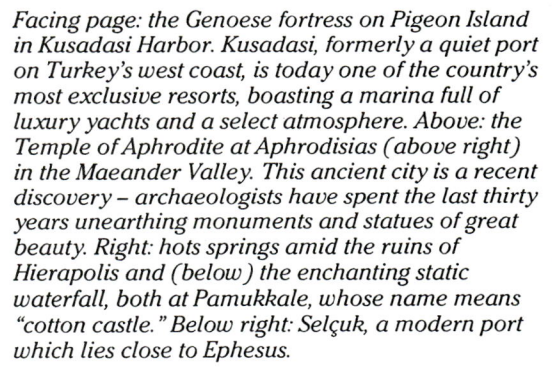

Facing page: the Genoese fortress on Pigeon Island in Kusadasi Harbor. Kusadasi, formerly a quiet port on Turkey's west coast, is today one of the country's most exclusive resorts, boasting a marina full of luxury yachts and a select atmosphere. Above: the Temple of Aphrodite at Aphrodisias (above right) in the Maeander Valley. This ancient city is a recent discovery – archaeologists have spent the last thirty years unearthing monuments and statues of great beauty. Right: hots springs amid the ruins of Hierapolis and (below) the enchanting static waterfall, both at Pamukkale, whose name means "cotton castle." Below right: Selçuk, a modern port which lies close to Ephesus.

Above and below: St. John's Basilica at Selçuk, which dominates the town from the top of a hill. The Basilica was built on the ruins of the old acropolis of Ephesus by the Emperor Justinian to honor the tomb of the Apostle John that is said to lie here under a marble slab. Left: the Gate of Persecution which leads to the Basilica. The South Aegean coast here is rich with ancient sites, such as the ruins of the Temple of Athena (above left) at Priene, the Temple of Apollo (below left), which dates from 300 AD, at Didyma, and the fourth century Roman theater (facing page bottom) at Miletus, south of Kusadasi. Facing page top: wildflowers in the countryside around Priene.

53

These pages and overleaf: Bodrum Harbor, dominated by a stalwart Crusader castle which stands on a peninsula just in front of the modern town. Today the South Aegean's prettiest resort, Bodrum dates from around 1000 BC when it was known as Halicarnassus. Here, in the third century BC one of the Seven Wonders of the World was constructed – the enormous white marble tomb of King Mausolus, built for him by his wife and sister. Known as the Mausoleum, today only the massive foundations remain; bricks from it were used by the Knights of St. John to build their Castle of St. Peter here in the fifteenth century. The Knights were only concerned with defending the castle from land attack – they were masters of the sea – so to enter the castle one passes through no less than seven gates. The four towers are named after the main languages the knights spoke: German, Italian French and English. The French tower, in the center of the citadel, is the highest and offers a superb view of the harbor. Today it houses a fascinating museum of underwater archaeology.

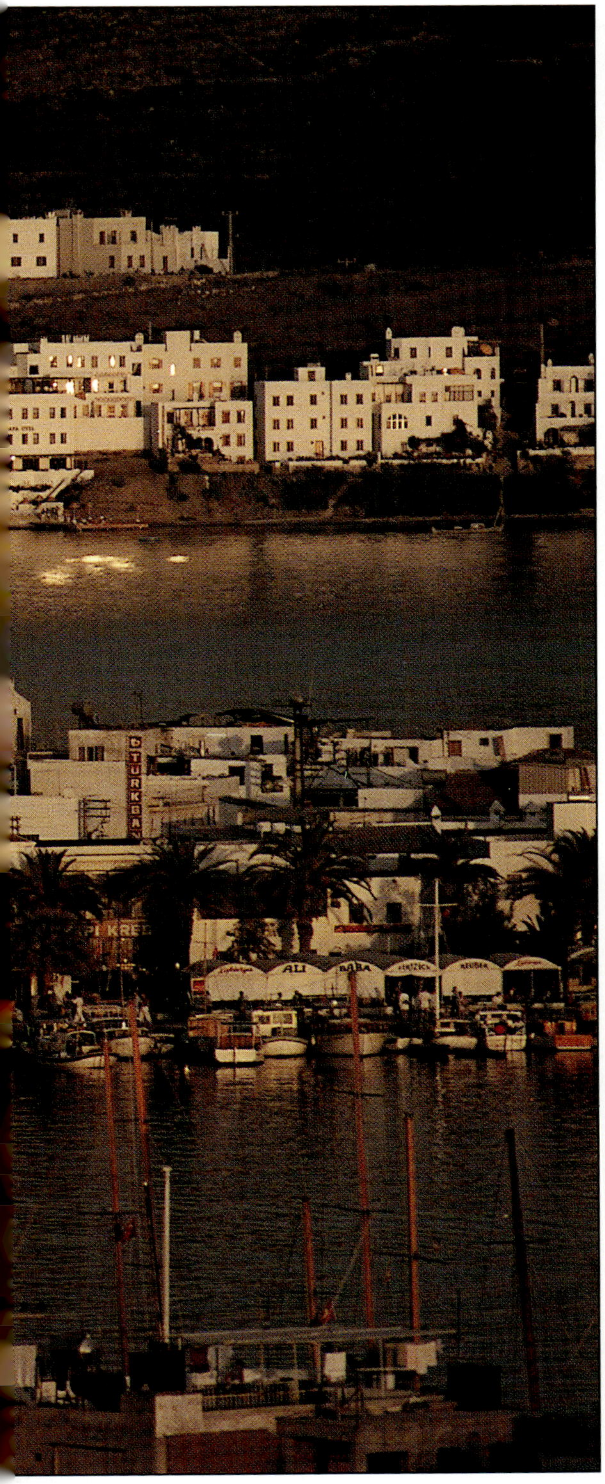
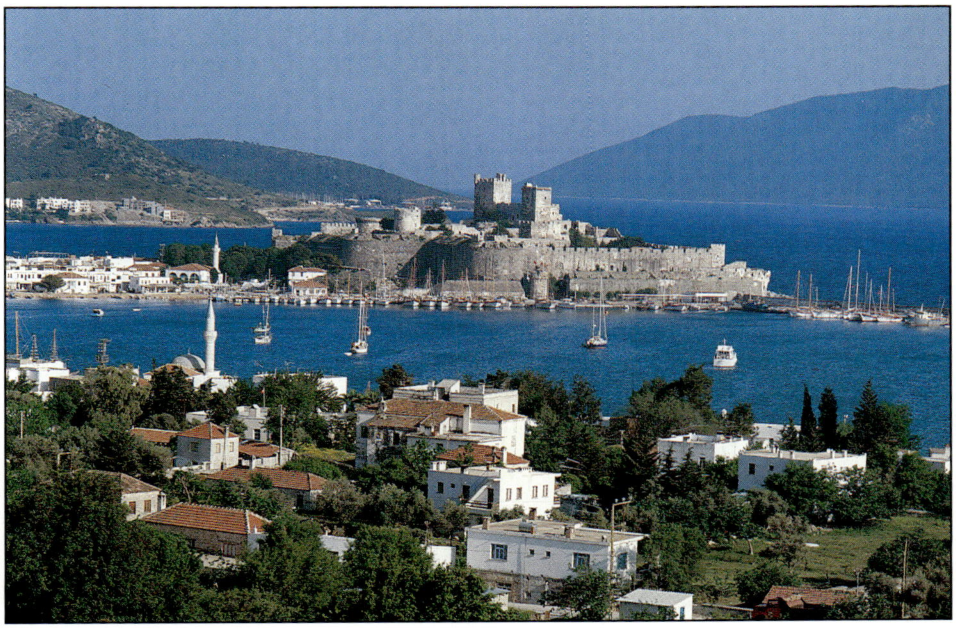
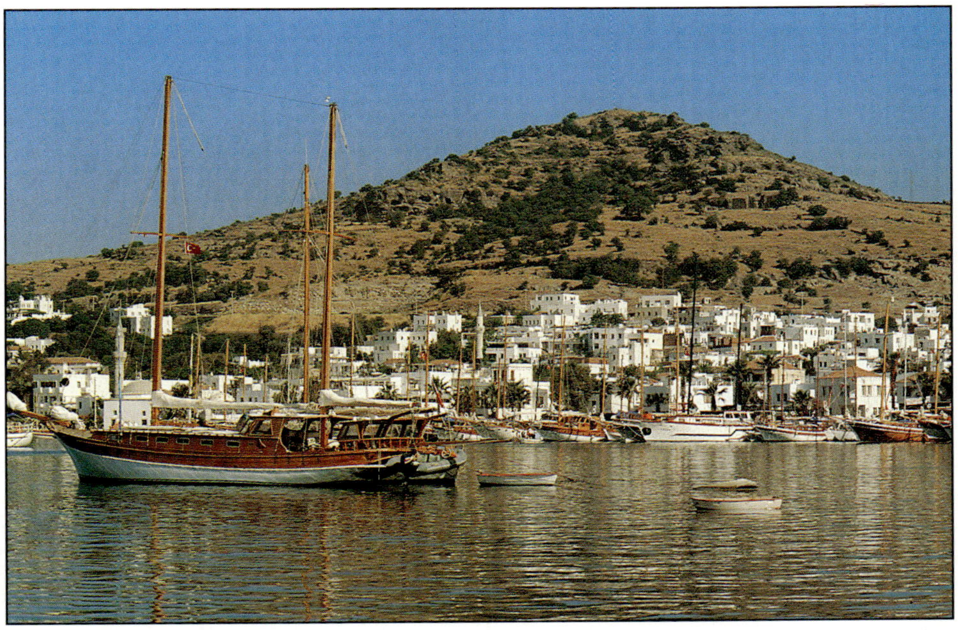
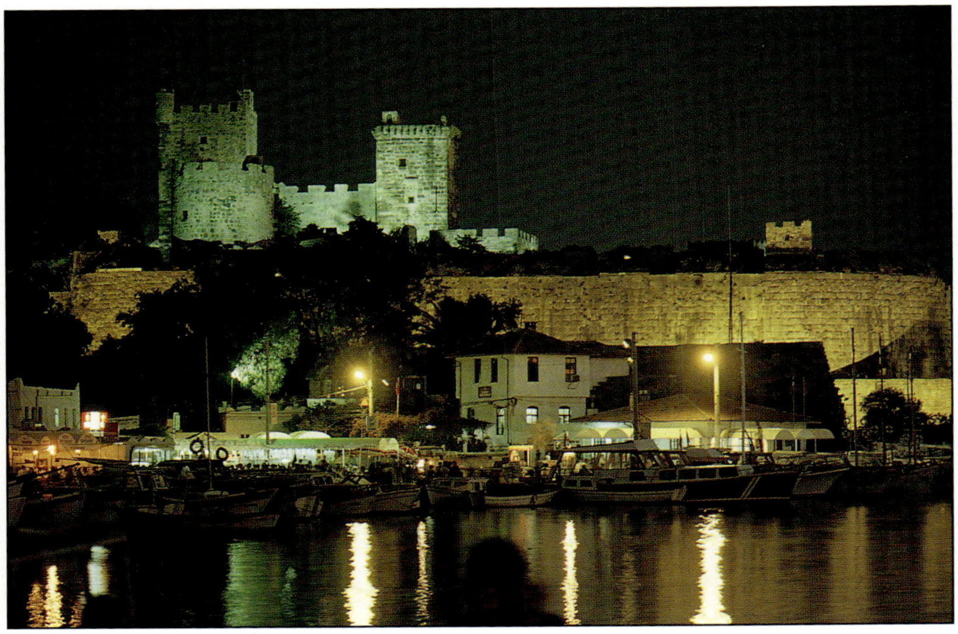

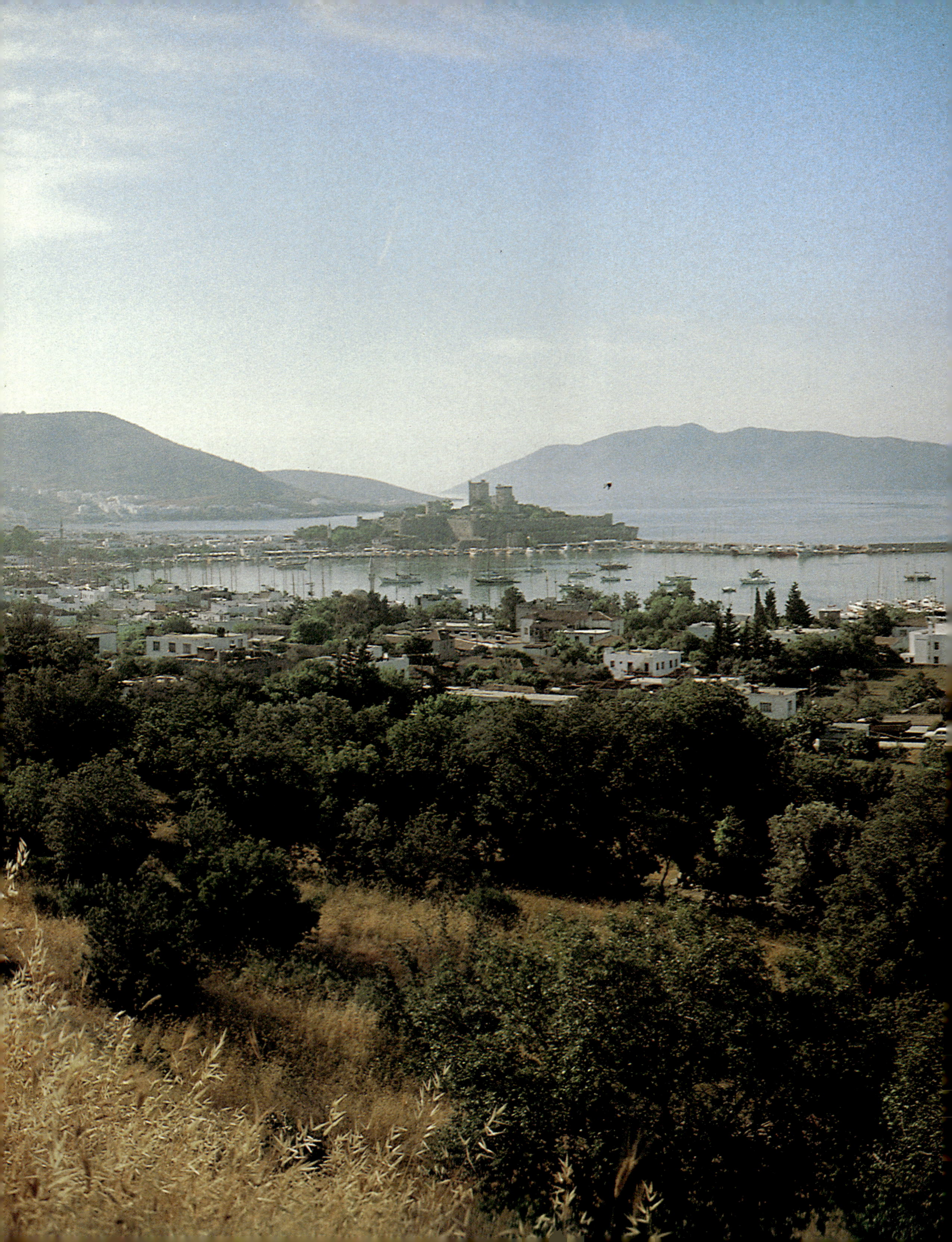

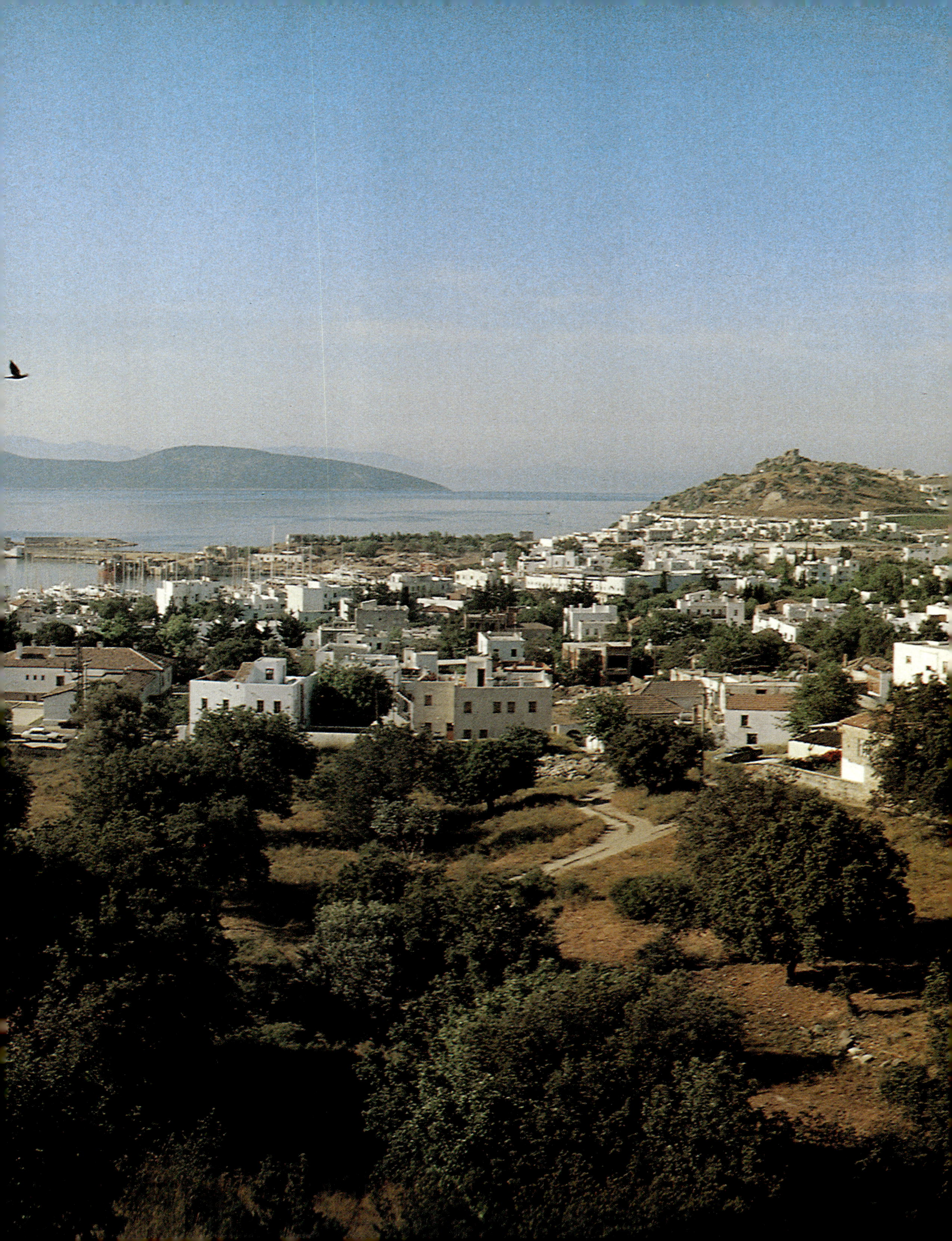

58

Left: a town on the Dalyan River (below left) in southwestern Turkey. The wooden structures in the river are fishing weirs. Bottom right: Kas, a small seaside village on the Mediterranean Sea that has blossomed into a quiet resort. In the center of town there is a fine Lycian tomb, known as the Monument Tomb, mounted on a high base. Once many such sarcophagi existed here, since the ancient Lycian town of Antiphellus lay not far from Kas. Most have been broken up for building materials, but some still stand on the sheer mountain wall that rises above the town and are illuminated at night. The Lycians were a maritime people who thrived in this district in the eighth century, living in a confederation of cities arrayed along this coast known as the Lycian League. They were later ruled by the Persians and then the Romans. Below: Kekova, a long offshore island that lies east of Kas. The countryside here is dotted with the ruins of ancient cities, and literally hundreds of Lycian tombs, some of them, somewhat bizarrely, lying partially submerged along the coast.

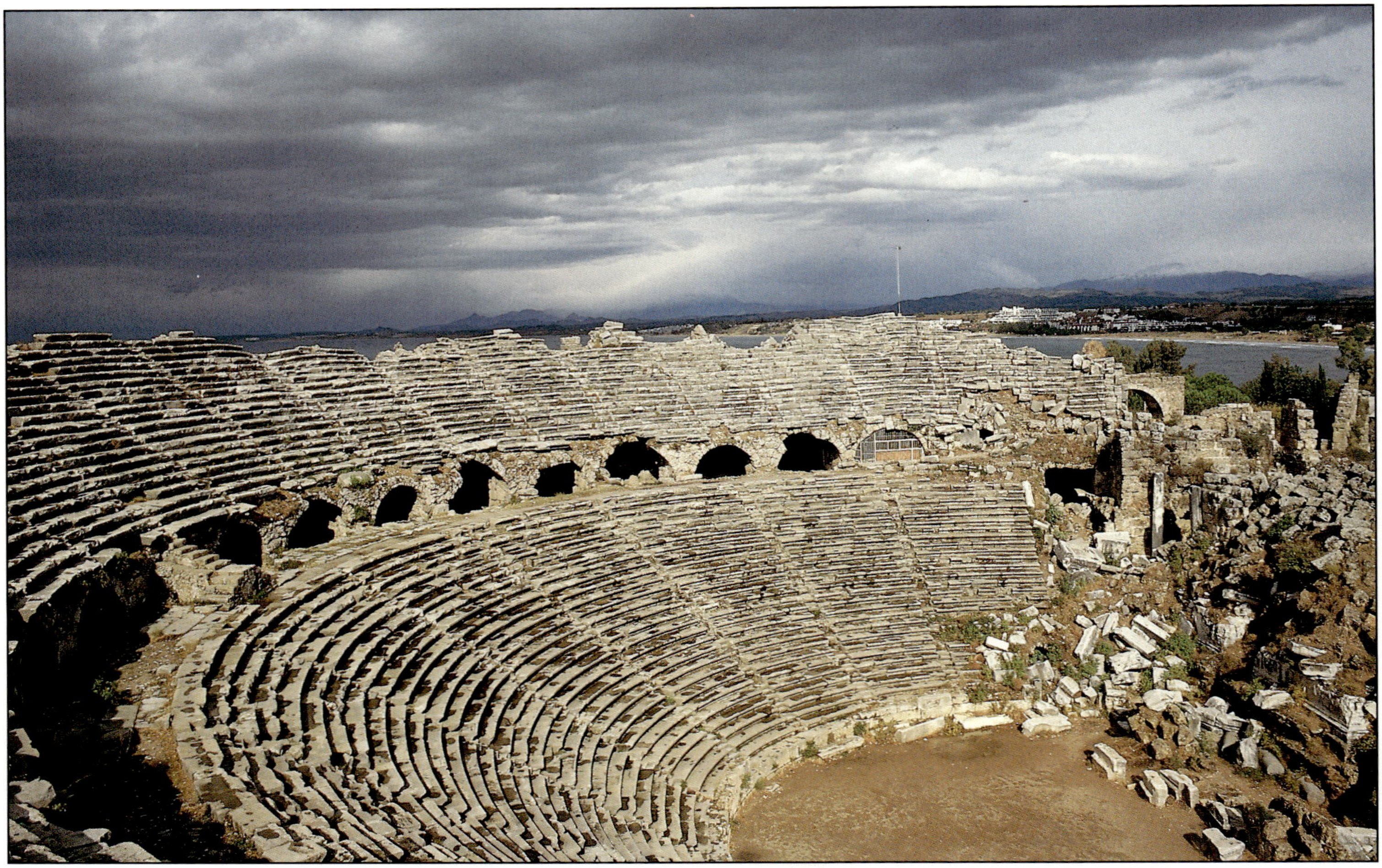

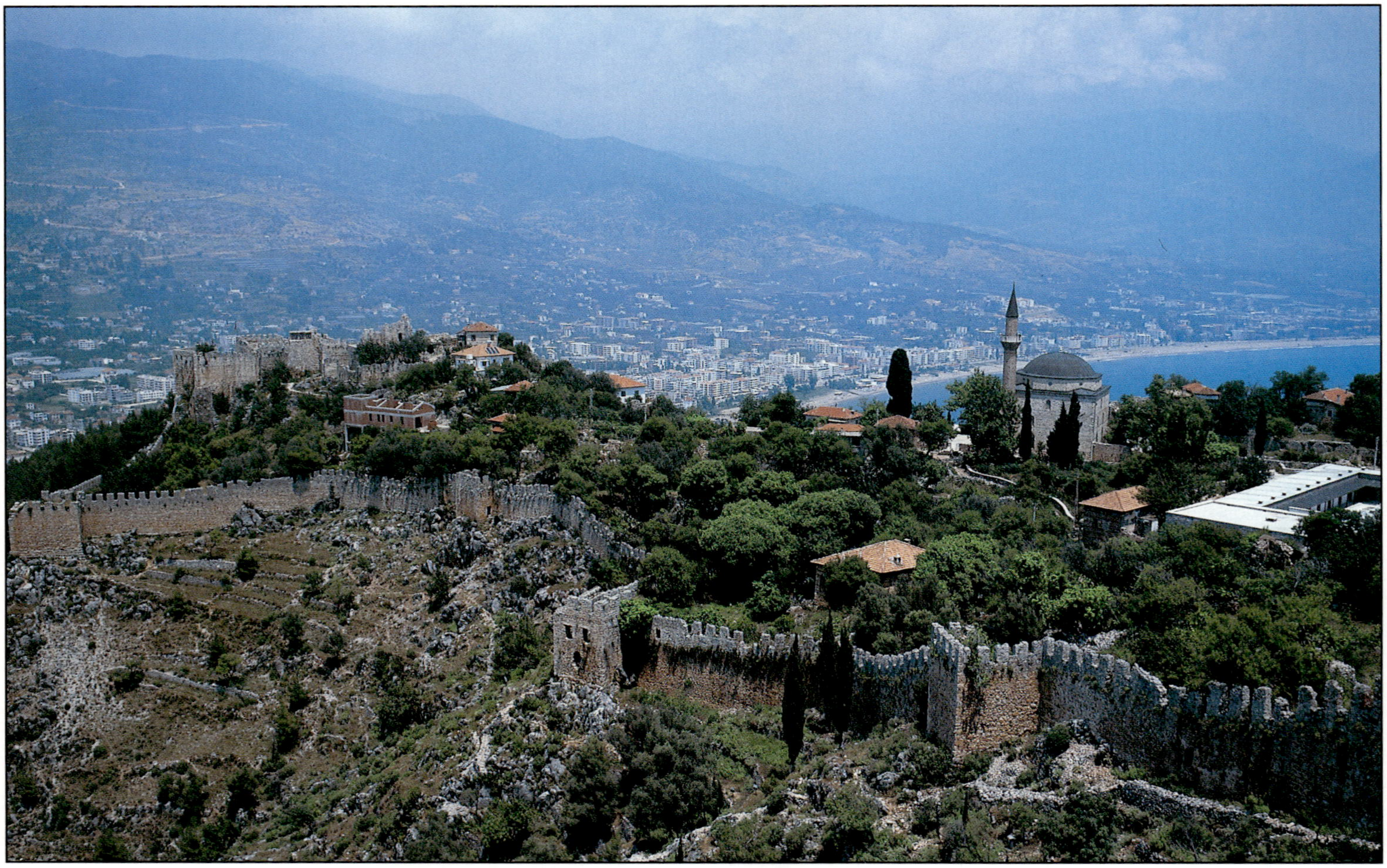

Facing page top: the Roman amphitheater at Side, built in the second century AD, and (facing page bottom, right and overleaf) Alanya, nicknamed "the pearl of the Turkish Mediterranean." Both towns lie on the south coast – Alanya is held to be the most beautiful. Above: tombs in the form of temple facades at Myra, also a south coast town. Most of the tombs here date from the fourth century BC. Below: the tomb of Amyntas at Fethiye. Below right: a Seljuk bridge spans the Eurymedon River near Aspendos and (above right) Antalya, which, like Alanya, lies on the Turkish Riviera. Following page: Turkish poppies.

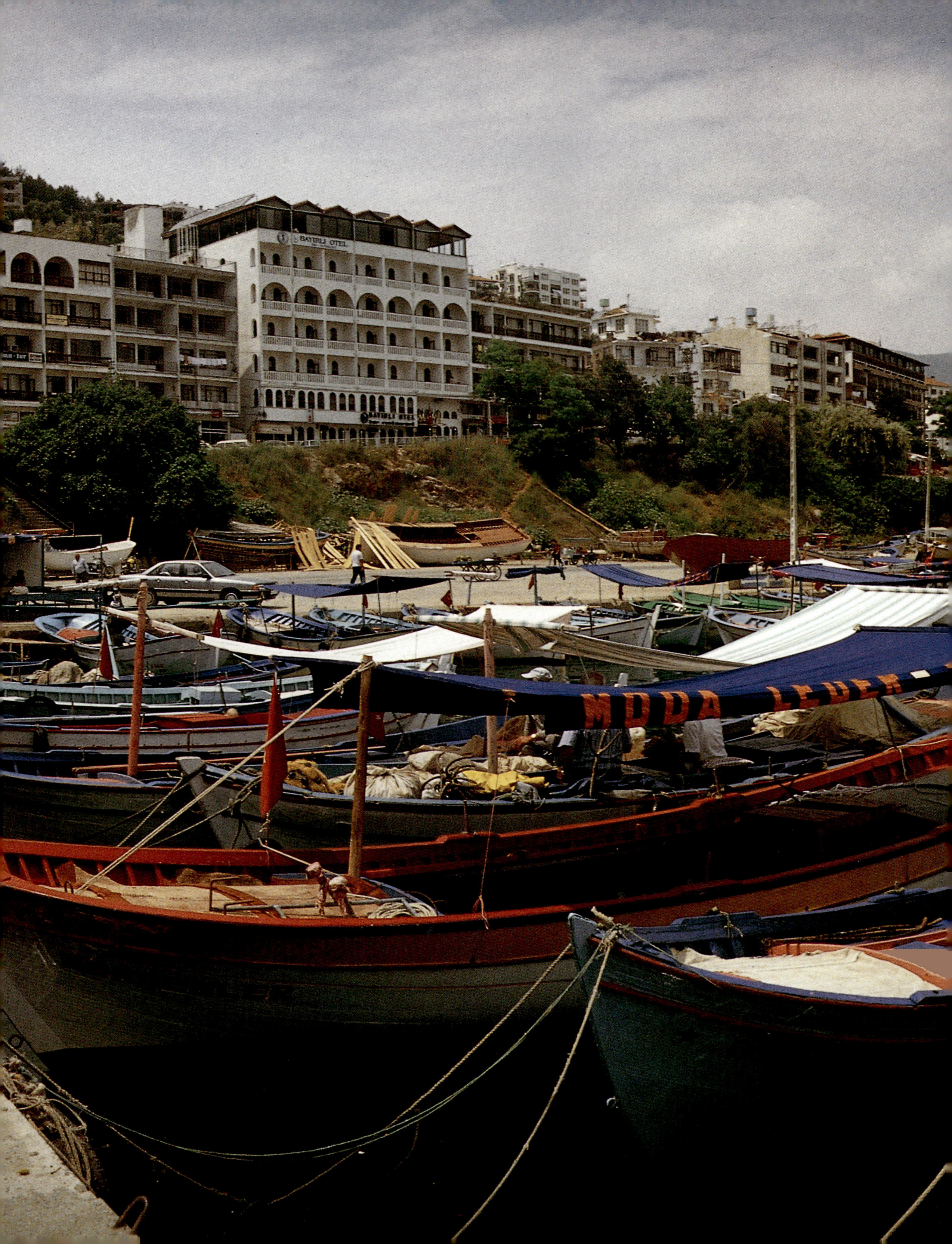